"Motherhood is not for the faint of and so are a mom's own temper ta finding other moms who will admit to what real life in the trenches looks like is always a relief. Becky is that kind of mom friend. She's been there, and she's going to give you real-life, practical advice for how to climb out. You're going to look around and discover the surprising secret that motherhood holds so much fun, buried right below the surface—all yours for the taking."

—Lisa-Jo Baker, bestselling author of *Never Unfriended* and *Surprised by Motherhood*

"If I'm being honest, more often than not I could wear the label 'Cranky Mom.' And I know for certain I'm not the only mom who struggles with this. In my online ministry to moms I have seen an overwhelming response any time we talk about anger. In *The Cranky Mom Fix*, Becky comes alongside us all to assure us we aren't alone and to help us find victory. With personal questions, assessments, and activities, this isn't just another book. It is a practical tool to help you get past the cranky once and for all!"

—Ruth Schwenk, founder of TheBetterMom.com and author of *The Better Mom*, *For Better or For Kids*, and *The Better Mom Devotional*

"If you've ever lost your cool with your kids and felt the pang of doubt and regret (and, really, who hasn't?), *The Cranky Mom Fix* is for you. Full of practical suggestions, biblical truth, and encouragement from one cranky mom to another, Becky's words will guide you to a place of joy as you parent, even on the most chaotic days."

—Teri Lynne Underwood, author of *Praying for Girls*

"With wit and wisdom, Becky helps us exchange our grumbles for grins and reclaim the joy that our homes and our hearts so desperately need. This book is an invitation to transformation. Don't miss it!"

—Alicia Bruxvoort, mom of five and member of the Proverbs 31 Ministries writing team

"In this book, Becky Kopitzke gives moms the practical tools to truly love and get the most out of every stage of motherhood."

—Jenny Rapson, founding editor of ForEveryMom.com

"Parenting certainly isn't simple, but it's much easier if you're equipped with support and encouragement! The pages of this book provide that and much more. Becky's stories and lessons have helped me fully appreciate the privilege of getting to know my children for the unique individuals God created them to be. I'm grateful for her gentle guidance about how to parent through tough issues with patience and courage, always pointing us toward God's wisdom."

—Courtney Westlake, author of *A Different Beautiful*

"Finally, here's a book that really can fix our mom problems. Becky Kopitzke has graciously offered practical tools, ideas, and perspectives to help fix the cranky in all of us. The momster in me devoured every tip, trick, and biblical truth, and I'm ready and equipped to tame this beast once and for all. This book is for every mom who wants and needs to build her home into a safe, enjoyable, and biblically based space for the entire family."

—Kristin Funston, Bible teacher and author of *More for Mom*

THE
Cranky
MOM FIX

Books by Becky Kopitzke

FROM BETHANY HOUSE PUBLISHERS

The Cranky Mom Fix
Generous Love

THE
Cranky
MOM FIX

Get a Happier, More Peaceful Home

by Slaying the *"Momster"* in All of Us

Becky Kopitzke

BETHANYHOUSE

a division of Baker Publishing Group
Minneapolis, Minnesota

© 2019 by Becky Kopitzke

Published by Bethany House Publishers
11400 Hampshire Avenue South
Bloomington, Minnesota 55438
www.bethanyhouse.com

Bethany House Publishers is a division of
Baker Publishing Group, Grand Rapids, Michigan

Printed in the United States of America

Library of Congress Cataloging-in-Publication Data

Names: Kopitzke, Becky, author.

Title: The cranky mom fix : get a happier, more peaceful home by slaying the "momster" in all of us / Becky Kopitzke.

Description: Minneapolis : Bethany House Publishers, a division of Baker Publishing Group, [2019] | Includes bibliographical references.

Identifiers: LCCN 2018053275| ISBN 9780764230547 (trade paper : alk. paper) | ISBN 9781493418794 (e-book)

Subjects: LCSH: Mothers—Psychology. | Parenting—Religious aspects. | Mother and child.

Classification: LCC HQ759 .K667 2019 | DDC 155.6/463—dc23

LC record available at https://lccn.loc.gov/2018053275

Cover design by Emily Weigel

Author represented by The Blythe Daniel Agency

In keeping with biblical principles of creation stewardship, Baker Publishing Group advocates the responsible use of our natural resources. As a member of the Green Press Initiative, our company uses recycled paper when possible. The text paper of this book is composed in part of post-consumer waste.

green press INITIATIVE

19 20 21 22 23 24 25   7 6 5 4 3 2 1

For Alisa

You always wore motherhood so beautifully

Contents

Be the F.U.N. Family   183

Introducing Monster Mom

There's this woman who shows up at my house sometimes. She's crabby, critical, self-centered, frazzled, and she throws better tantrums than my toddlers ever did.

My children call her Monster Mom. *Momster* for short.

Sadly, she looks a lot like me.

We all hate her.

I remember the first time Monster Mom arrived—unannounced, uninvited, as she always does. My firstborn daughter was only three weeks old. Precious baby girl had the audacity to wake up screaming and demanding a diaper change *again* for what seemed like the hundredth time in only seven days. So with eyeballs burning from exhaustion and hormonal tears, I rose, stumbled to the nursery, scooped my bundle from her crib, and placed her gently on the changing table. She stared up at me with those glossy saucers, wide awake and needy. I sniffed—and my nostrils were accosted by the stench of a blowout diaper. We're talking 2 a.m., full-body bath, start from scratch with a new onesie, whoa momma, throw the old one away.

That was the moment something in me snapped and my sensible soul gave way to the Momster possessor. She opened her mouth and growled—actually *growled*, Lord have mercy—at a helpless, beautiful, ginger-haired infant, my treasure from God.

"Grrrr!!! Why won't you let me sleep? Mommy is so tired!!!"

Suddenly, as if someone had slapped me on the cheek, the sound of my own voice startled me and I crumpled over the changing table in a ball of weeping shame. I stroked my baby's fingers and cried, *I'm sorry, I'm sorry, I'm sorry.* Monster Mom had crept in and thwacked us both hard.

I wanted to strangle the blasted witch.

Unfortunately, though, she kept showing up. Over the years as my baby grew and became a big sister, Monster Mom gained twice the strength and cause for rebellion. Now she faced two children, two different personalities, two harried schedules to keep, and one worn-out mother body that just could not resist the overpowering urge to blow. Through sibling squabbles, disobedience, and back talk, not to mention those daily episodes of pushing my dawdling children out the door while barking classic parenting lines such as *"I told you to put your shoes on"* and *"School doesn't wait for us, people!"* it came to pass that Monster Mom upgraded from visitor to resident, leasing a long-term agreement with my heart.

She burst on the scene whenever my kids bickered, begged, belly-ached, or whined.

She erupted from my lungs each time a Hula-Hoop popped me in the forehead. Or a Nerf bullet. Or somebody's foot.

And she greeted my sweet children if they woke before sunrise insisting Oreos make good breakfast food. Of course, Oreos are fantastic any time of day—if you're the mother. But everybody knows children shouldn't eat cookies for breakfast, right? Or can they? What would a good mom do in this situation?

If I didn't know the answer, Monster Mom did.

And I resented her for it every time.

Do you resent her, too?

Then listen close. I have good news for you, my friend. It just might be the very encouragement you've been desperate to hear.

I got rid of her.

That's right. Monster Mom doesn't live with me anymore. I'm proud to say I tossed her out on her prickly behind, and she has not unpacked her bags in my house since. Oh, she threatens to squeeze through the window from time to time, but now I know how to keep her out. I'm wise to her devices and have learned—the hard way—what it takes to beat them.

Do you want to know, too?

How can an ordinary, God-fearing woman manage to defeat that cantankerous beast who wears her clothes and steals her voice and crushes her child's spirit?

Is it actually possible to be gentle, patient, and unconditionally kind—even when the kiddos aren't?

And how in the world can we break the cycle of disobedience, punishment, frustration, and regret?

Ah. The answers lie in the pages of this book. And I'm so happy you've joined me here.

If you know Monster Mom like I know Monster Mom, if she invades your home and your aching heart, too, then *welcome*, sister. You have come to the right place. Together, over these next many chapters, we are going to discover how to tame that nasty Momster and reclaim true peace for your soul. It's going to be a beautiful transformation; I know this firsthand.

You will be kinder. You will be softer. You will enjoy your children more than you scold them.

And the entire family will reap the benefits.

Are you ready? I cannot wait to begin.

Taming the Momster

"Abominable! That's what they called me! Don't you think that's a little harsh? I mean, how about the *Adorable* Snowman?" —*Monsters, Inc.*

1

Who's the Real Enemy Here?

Bedtime is my favorite time of day. The house is quiet, we gather around the bunk bed to say family prayers, then my husband and I tuck our two school-age daughters snug under their covers before retreating to the family room for an hour of grown-up reading, Netflix, or snacks nobody begs to share. Ahhhhh. Peaceful, right?

It's the ten minutes *before* bedtime that break me.

Can we stay up a little later, pleeeease, Mom?

But I don't want to brush my teeth!

I'm still hungry. I want a snack!

She's bumping into me! I can't wash my face when she's bumping into me!

Oh, Mom, can you sign my homework and get me a glass of water and find my book and my flashlight and, hey, I don't have any clean socks for tomorrow, can you wash some quick, please? Plus, um, I kind of forgot to tell you . . . I have a spelling test in the morning and I haven't studied for it. Sorry.

Heaven help me. At the end of the day, I feel less like a mom and more like a wild horse tamer. *Do this, don't do that, just CO-OPERATE already, dear children,* and maybe we wouldn't have to battle each other's wills night upon night. After nagging my girls to put on their pajamas, set out tomorrow's clothing, brush their hair, and floss their teeth—which you'd think I shouldn't have to tell them in the first place, since we do this *every single night*—a certain thought creeps into my head and threatens to park there.

If only my children would behave—then I wouldn't have to be such a crank!

Have you thought that, too?

Whose Fault Is It?

When the Momster arrives, it's easy to blame the kids for letting her in. I mean, there has to be a cause behind our exasperation, right? It must be because the children disobeyed, dragged their feet, didn't listen, wouldn't share. It's all their fault, I tell you! Show me a cranky mom and I'll show you a kid who made her that way.

Except, as my grandmother used to say, that's a bunch of bologna.

Our kids don't make us cranky.

We do.

The first step to taming the Momster is knowing who your real enemy is. It's not your kids. They're on your team. According to the Bible, the real culprit is your very own heart: "The heart is deceitful above all things and beyond cure. Who can understand it?" (Jeremiah 17:9).

Human hearts are unreliable. They lie to us. Until the day we reach heaven, our hearts are contaminated with original sin—impatience, irritability, selfishness, folly. So when circumstances threaten to draw those sins to the surface, our faulty hearts would have us believe *feeling* cranky requires *acting* cranky. We think we have no choice.

But we do.

> Above all else, guard your heart, for everything you do flows from it.
>
> Proverbs 4:23

Choose Love

When my younger daughter was two, she discovered she could pitter-patter out of her toddler bed, trip the threshold from bedroom to hallway, and roam free. At which point she viewed nap time as merely optional.

"Go back to your room. It's time to sleep." I stood at the baby gate with fists on my hips and my mouth screwed tight. My daughter clasped the gate with both hands and batted her lashes.

"No!" A half-smile teetered on her lips. I stepped over the gate, wrapped her fingers in mine, and led her back to bed.

"Sweet dreams." I pulled a blanket over her limbs and left the room. Three seconds later she yanked her covers off and followed me down the hall.

"Go back to bed." We resumed our standoff at the gate. "I am not joking."

"No!" she barked.

"Okay, that's your choice. You're on your own now." I spun on my heels and stomped out of sight toward the family room.

A moment later, I heard a whimper in the hallway. Then a rattling sound. *Crash! Boom!* I ran through the kitchen to find my toddler scampering toward me. The little stinker had busted down the baby gate!

"That's it, young lady!" Anger burned into my temples and blew steam out my ears. "I'm throwing away your stuffed animals!"

Like a mad woman, I huffed from room to room, swiping every fuzzy dog and bunny in my path. When my arms were stacked with plush toys, I sped toward the garbage can. My daughter wailed at my heels, and the Momster gave me a fuming pep talk.

She wants a fight? I'll show her a fight. Pure defiance, that's all this is. Stay strong. She needs to learn to obey. It's my job to teach her! To discipline! To establish authority! If I fail to squash nap-time arguments, what's next? Breaking curfew? Robbing banks? Heaven help me, I will not let my child grow up to be an outlaw!

"Mommy, I want you!"

What did she say?

"Muh-muh-mommy! I-I-I! Want! You!" Gulping for air between sobs, my daughter sputtered this desperate plea.

Not "Stop." Not "No, don't throw away doggie." Again she hiccupped, *"Mommy, I want you!"*

What kind of outlaw says that?

I froze, turned around, and released the stuffed animals into a heap on the floor. My baby girl's cheeks were streaked pink with tears. She lifted her open palms to my waist.

"Mommy," she whispered now. "I want you to hold me."

Instantly my anger deflated and I slumped down to grab her. She nestled her head in my shoulder and closed her eyes. I clutched her warm body to mine, kissed her spongy cheek, and rocked. Within two minutes, she fell asleep in my arms.

My daughter wasn't looking for a fight after all. Quite the opposite—she wanted love.

Booger. What had I given her instead? Rules. Rants. Scolding. The Momster was so bent on showing the kiddo who's boss, I lost sight of that fundamental need to let love lead my actions.

Loving parents set limits, yes. We must respond to rebellion with consistency and a firm stance. I get that. But sometimes I act very unloving when I lay down the law. Biblically speaking, the law was always meant to point us to Jesus. And Jesus embodies love.

> Above all, love each other deeply, because love covers over a multitude of sins.
>
> 1 Peter 4:8

You and I are raising families, not military units. So before we lash out in angry discipline, consider we have a choice: law or love.

Yes, sometimes love looks tough, like a time-out or taking the keys away. "Because the Lord disciplines those he loves, as a father the son he delights in" (Proverbs 3:12). But more often I think love can look like hugs, tender words, and respect for the stuffed-animal kingdom.

It is entirely possible to feel frustrated without resorting to *acting* frustrated. The first step is deciding whose side you're on.

"The Devil Made Me Do It"

As Christians, wholly surrendered to Jesus, we serve a victorious Savior. Jesus already defeated Satan when He won the battle for our souls on the cross. So I don't put a lot of stock in the devil's schemes. He's a loser and he'll only ever be a loser. However, that doesn't erase the fact that he's still out there.

> For our struggle is not against flesh and blood, but against the rulers, against the authorities, against the powers of this dark world and against the spiritual forces of evil in the heavenly realms.
>
> Ephesians 6:12

Does that sound spooky to you? Let's unpack it a bit.

"For our struggle is not against flesh and blood . . ." That means people (i.e., our children). Once again, our kids are not the enemy.

". . . but against the rulers, against the authorities, against the powers of this dark world and against the spiritual forces of evil in the heavenly realms." That would be Satan and his loser cronies. Yes, demons are a real thing, and God warns us to be on guard, ready to defend ourselves against their lies and temptations. Even the staunchest believers can trip up if we're not careful. But thankfully we don't have to do it alone, nor do we have to be afraid. God gives us the wisdom, power, and protection to face anything the devil throws our way.

> Therefore put on the full armor of God, so that when the day of evil comes, you may be able to stand your ground, and after you have done everything, to stand. Stand firm then, with the belt of truth buckled around your waist, with the breastplate of righteousness in place, and with your feet fitted with the readiness that comes from the gospel of peace. In addition to all this, take up the shield

21

of faith, with which you can extinguish all the flaming arrows of the evil one.

Ephesians 6:13–16

Faith is key to defeating the Momster. Our hearts are prone to believing the devil's claims that cranky is okay, it's normal, it's therapeutic. But God knows better. He is the definition of love (1 John 4:8), so it's no wonder Satan wants us to act anything but loving. Don't let the enemy win. Choose whose side you're on and stick to it. Faith in Jesus wins every time.

You Are Responsible for You

Why do we harp on our kids? Why do we set rules and correct their behavior and follow them around the house barking at them to pick up their socks and apologize to their sister? For many of us, the root is much deeper than a mood. Underneath it all, we simply, desperately want our kids to turn out okay. And perhaps we fear they won't.

As moms we feel enormous pressure to produce "good" children, do we not? We want our kids to listen in school and make wise friends and grow up to be the kind of adults who work hard and pay their bills and go to church on Sunday. Naturally we're deeply concerned about their development, their behavior, their obedience while they're still under Mom and Dad's roof, while we have the chance to mold them and shape them and teach them right from wrong. It's our job, right?! It's all up to us! I mean, isn't our children's success or failure in life actually a reflection on our performance as parents?

Well . . . not entirely.

Mostly not.

Our children belong to God first, and it's true we do have a responsibility to raise them right, to "bring them up in the training and instruction of the Lord" (Ephesians 6:4). There are examples in the Old Testament of parents whose wrongdoing led to a child's demise, and God did indeed hold the parent responsible. We'll talk more about that later.

Yet ultimately, regardless of our parenting prowess (or lack thereof), we cannot make our children's choices for them. They are individuals with their own free will, their own unique DNA, and their own God-ordained internal wiring, which may or may not download everything we've been programming into them since the day they were born.

We can train them to obey. But we cannot obey for them.

We can demonstrate how to love. But we cannot love for them.

We can teach them to follow Jesus and live out our own faith in front of their beloved faces every day of their childhood. But we cannot choose Jesus for them. And if you ask me, that is the greatest kicker in all the universe.

What more could I possibly want for my kids than a saving relationship with the one true God? And yet it is the one thing I cannot give them. They must choose it for themselves.

As parents, we do the prep work. We pour our sweaty souls into the job of raising godly kids. But in the end, the result is not up to us. Our children will make choices, some wise and some not, and in the end their lives are also not their own.

They belong to God.

And He decides who they will become. Not us.

> In their hearts humans plan their course, but the Lord establishes their steps.
>
> Proverbs 16:9

The very best we can do for our children is to point them to Jesus and pray they will grab hold of Him. Meanwhile, in our quest to train and disciple our kids, let's make sure we're not diluting our own witness by defaulting to those ugly Momster habits. One day, when this life transcends and we stand before God in heaven, He will not ask us if our kids are riding our coattails. They are responsible for their own salvation. And we are responsible for ours.

> For we must all appear before the judgment seat of Christ, so that each of us may receive what is due us for the things done while in the body, whether good or bad.
>
> 2 Corinthians 5:10

 *Let's Dig In!*

> Take delight in the Lord, and he will give you the desires of your heart.
>
> Psalm 37:4

The Bible is the central tool in our Cranky Mom Fix toolbox. The better you get acquainted with your Bible, the more you'll discover who God is, what He asks of you, and how His truth and grace can help you slay the Momster. The closer you grow to God, the more your desires will become like His. In other words, you'll want for yourself whatever God wants for you. And that is a powerful way to live.

At the end of each chapter, I encourage you to spend some time digging into the Bible to learn more about the concepts we explored in these pages. The following questions are designed to make it easy for you to align your personal Bible time with what you're learning in this book. You might want to keep an accompanying journal or notebook to record your answers and reflections.

The Cranky Mom Fix is a helpful guide, but nothing compares to God's original Good Book. His words are so much smarter than mine. Let's dig in.

1. Read Jeremiah 17:9. According to that verse, what adjective best describes the human heart?

   God's Word says the heart is *deceitful* above all things. Has your heart ever led you astray? Think of a time you made a poor decision because your emotions influenced your actions. The first step to taming the Momster is recognizing that our *feelings* cannot be trusted to guide our behavior. God's truth can. That's why we must place God's truth above our cranky emotions in the heat of the moment. In the next several chapters, we're going to discuss a series of practical strategies to do just that.

2. *Deceit* means to misrepresent or conceal the truth. Read John 8:44. Who is the Father of Lies? When we allow our heart's frustrations to spew onto our children, we are essentially believing the enemy's lies, such as:

   • I'll feel better if I yell.

   • All moms get cranky, so it must be an acceptable part of the job.

   • I deserve to be left alone. (See Romans 6:23 and Psalm 103:10. What do we really deserve?)

3. One of my favorite verses in the Bible is Proverbs 14:1: "The wise woman builds her house, but with her own hands the foolish one tears hers down." What are you hoping to "build" in your house/family? Write a list of benefits or godly traits, such as, "I'm hoping to build . . . *honesty, integrity, acceptance, kindness, gentleness.*" Now review that list and determine which areas you believe are currently lacking most.

4. What does it take to be a "wise woman"? See Proverbs 1:7 and 19:20. What/who is our source of wisdom? God and His Word! We can gain this wisdom several ways, including:

   • Studying the Bible (which you are doing right now!)

   • Seeking out wise counselors and mentors

- Praying! See James 1:5. Pray for God to grant you wisdom and to reveal any blind spots in your behavior that may be foolish rather than wise.

5. Read 1 Corinthians 10:12. In what ways can we get too comfortable in our faith or family life? Have you ever assumed you're not susceptible to the devil's temptations? How does this verse challenge your thinking? Revisit Ephesians 6:10–17 and ask God to give you a renewed passion for protecting your heart.

6. Read 1 Samuel 2:12–36. This passage tells the story of Eli, whose sons were wicked and offended the Lord by abusing their office as priests. Eli loved God and hated evil, yet he failed to raise godly sons. Therefore, God punished the whole family, including Eli.

At first blush this appears to contradict our discussion about parents and children being held responsible for themselves before God. However, a deeper look into this passage reveals Eli was a passive parent. He did not follow God's instructions to train his sons in the Lord. Indeed, we see he made three grave mistakes:

- *Failure to discern.* Eli confronted his sons only after he learned about their bad behavior from other people. He never detected it himself. As parents we ought to be watchful, devoting the time and attention necessary to know what our children are doing and believing. Eli did not; therefore, God held him accountable for this error.
- *Failure to discipline.* Even after confronting his sons, Eli did not discipline them for their actions. A loving, intentional parent will exercise his or her authority to correct and redirect a child's poor choices.
- *Failure to divide.* Finally, after Eli's sons continued down their wayward path, Eli failed to draw a line between what he stood for and what his sons stood for.

The lines were blurred. He knew his sons were disrespecting the house of God, and yet he allowed them to continue serving as priests. As people of God, our kids must know where we stand on topics of moral value. We can still love them, but we must cease to enable their poor choices. In the end, God held Eli responsible not for his inability to guide his sons, but for his *unwillingness* to do so.[1]

What does this tell you about God's call on your life as a mom? What are we responsible for? What are we not responsible for?

7. If you read through the Old Testament accounts of Israel's kings and judges, often a ruler's mother is named. In an age when women were typically held in lower esteem, this is remarkable. Why do you think the Bible cites mothers? What does this say about our role in the family and in God's kingdom as a whole?

8. See Psalm 51:10 and James 3:8. Who is the only One with the power to transform your heart and tame the Momster? (Hint: It's not you or me!) That, sweet mom, is why you are reading this book. Together we are seeking God's wisdom and guidance for real help and lasting change that only He can give!

2

What Are Your Triggers?

You know how some women are just made to nurture newborns? They revel in snuggling and nursing and cooing to their sweet babies. They treasure those fleeting weeks of infancy spent rocking a teeny one to sleep. They wear their precious bundles on their chests, wrapped up tight in Houdini-style cloth carriers while they wash dishes or cheer for their older children on the soccer field. When I see these ladies, looking all rested and lovely on two hours of sleep, I wonder how they defy the laws of nature and under-eye circles. I mean, *sleepless* is just another word for *haggard*, right? But these women are beautiful. They're magic.

I am not one of them.

Sleep deprivation is like poison to me, body and soul. I spent the first six months of both of my daughters' lives in a bloodshot brain fog, and ever since, any time I'm forced to function on fewer than six hours of sleep, I feel like scratching my eyeballs out—and yours.

Because when I'm tired, I'm cranky. Fatigue is one of my biggest triggers for conjuring the Momster. I know this about myself now, so when I'm running on less than a full tank of gas, I put a few safeties in place to prevent a total wreck. We'll talk about those in a bit.

First, let's identify some of the most common cranky triggers. Do you know what yours are? A crucial step in disarming the Momster is becoming aware of what summons her in the first place. Only then can we address those triggers and prevent them from wreaking havoc on our homes.

What Trips Your Cranky Threshold?

As busy, intentional, and desperately mortal parents, we all face a series of pressures, both internal and external. Not every woman battles every trigger, and some struggle more than others, but in general I've found our cranky triggers fall into five categories. How many of these can you relate to?

1. Physical

God created our bodies, and they are intricate works of art. However, we live in a post-Eden world where nothing is perfect; therefore, these "jars of clay" in which our souls reside do have certain limits (see 2 Corinthians 4:7). It's all too easy to get cranky when we're dealing with factors like these:

Fatigue

Hunger

Pain (headache, cramps, backache, etc.)

Illness

Lacking coffee/caffeine

Medication effects

Hormones

Too hot/too cold

Other: What would you add?

2. Emotional

Just as God created our bodies, He also created our souls. He made us emotional beings, and that's generally a good thing. Sometimes, though—as many of us know well—we ladies can get a little wacko in the emotions department.

Emotional triggers are often related to the physical triggers we just listed. Some days we can't even tell which came first—the worry or the pain, the exhaustion or the stress. For crying out loud, why can't we just blame it on the kids and eat a bag of chips, right?

We'll be exploring plenty of ways to take responsibility for our emotions in the chapters ahead. For now I just want you to recognize these triggers when they rear their ugly heads.

Worry, anxiety

Feeling down or depressed

Grief, heartache, disappointment

Conflict with spouse

Feeling underappreciated or neglected

Job stress

In-law stress

Caregiver stress (aging parents, sick children)

Other: What would you add?

3. Environmental

Our physical and emotional limitations often rub up against triggers in our surroundings, making kindness and self-control especially difficult to muster. I confess these are some of my toughest triggers. How about you?

Feeling too busy, distracted, or overwhelmed

Surrounded by too much noise or activity

Feeling rushed or running late

Surrounded by mess or disorganization

Crummy weather

Sudden change in routine, interruptions (flat tire, vomiting child, etc.)

Other: What would you add?

4. Spiritual

Without a doubt, a healthy spiritual life is the most important defense against the Momster. When we neglect our relationship with God, not only do all the other triggers appear amplified, but we also lack the power and wisdom to fight them off. Many a cranky moment could be prevented if we'd learn to manage these triggers.

Neglecting prayer

Neglecting Bible study/reading

Avoiding fellowship and accountability with other Christians

Empty tank (not enough "me" time)

Other: What would you add?

5. Child's Behavior

Finally, let's acknowledge that in many situations, the kids do prompt our ugliness. Certain behaviors and decisions our children make can mobilize the Momster faster than my dog can chase a squirrel, yet we must remember the true culprit is always our own heart's response. We'll spend quite a bit of time exploring what to do about that in the pages to come. For now, here's a list of some common grievances among us flustered moms. Sisters, can I get an amen?

Whining

Bickering/sibling conflict

Begging

Crying

Ignoring instructions

Disobeying/defiance

Dawdling

Interrupting

Constant requests for help or attention

Meltdowns in public

Irresponsibility/poor choices

Other: What would you add?

Keep a Record of Your Triggers

Now that we've pinpointed some of the factors that trip us up, it's important to become students of our own behavior. When you act cranky, ask yourself—why? What's causing this? It's okay if you feel powerless to change it at this point; keep reading, and you soon won't. Right now the goal is to become aware of what's prompting your crankiness. Only then can you tackle a known adversary and win.

— What Are My Triggers? —

Today and every day for the next few weeks, I challenge you to keep a record of your triggers. Use the handy "What Are My Triggers?" sheet found in the Tools and Resources section in the back of this book. Make copies or download a printable version at beckykopitzke.com/crankymomfix. Be diligent about this if you can. The purpose is to become so familiar with your triggers that you're able to preempt them with the insights and strategies we'll be learning.

What to Do When a Trigger Is Tripped

Besides sleep deprivation, another of my triggers is work stress. When I'm under a tight writing deadline or consumed by a new project, I tend to develop tunnel vision for the task. Unfortunately, that means my priorities twist and I start viewing my kids as a distraction rather than my purpose. This problem is magnified by the fact that I work from home, where all the happy, noisy family activity surrounds me—and have I mentioned I share an office with my tween daughter?!

When I find myself snapping at my beloved people because I'm under pressure from obligations that have nothing to do with them—poor innocent children (and husband and dog)—I know what I've got to do. Here are some general rules I keep in mind when my triggers are tripped and the Momster looms.

Acknowledge the culprit. Identify your trigger. Give it a name. This helps us recognize the root of our crankiness and makes it possible to see ourselves from the outside looking in.

Hmmm . . . why do I feel like throwing this hairbrush right now? Well, I have a headache, and I'm still upset over that argument I had with my husband this morning. Okay then, moving on.

Ultimately, the goal is to call out our triggers *before* we react, but at first that may not happen. Give yourself grace and remember your behavior is actually a symptom of what's happening in your heart—and thankfully God is in the business of repairing hearts.

> Create in me a pure heart, O God, and renew a steadfast spirit within me.
>
> Psalm 51:10

Be honest. Kids are perceptive; they can tell when we're crabby. Worst-case scenario, they'll blame themselves for our moods, fearing Mom's approval hinges on their performance. That's certainly not the message we want to send to our kids. So simply fess up, shift the weight of responsibility to your own shoulders, and

—— Heart to Heart Q&A ——

As we begin *The Cranky Mom Fix*, I encourage you to establish a baseline understanding of your mom role—from your child's point of view. If your kids are old enough to talk, invite them to have an honest discussion about your relationship. Allow them to share their perspective of who you are and how you treat them. I've been humbled many times by these conversations, yet so grateful to my children for shining a light on my blind spots. We may think we know where we need to improve, but seeing ourselves from our children's eyes can give us a fuller, more accurate picture of the crank within—and of the loving mom within, too.

One important rule: You must assure your children that you will *not* get angry with them for being honest. Open communication and transparency—free from the fear of condemnation—are key assets in a loving home environment. No matter what you hear, do not get defensive or argue. The idea is to show your children that you care about how they feel.

Some of these questions/answers may be obvious to you, but remember you're prompting your child's perspectives, not imposing your own perspectives on your child. Ask and be willing to listen. Finally, if appropriate, apologize for any hurt feelings or fear your child

empower your children to be part of the solution. For example, I might say to my girls, "Mom is really tired right now, and that makes me more prone to being impatient. I'm going to pray for God to help me. Can you also help me out by treating each other kindly while you play that game, please?"

> Then I acknowledged my sin to you and did not cover up my iniquity. I said, "I will confess my transgressions to the Lord." And you forgave the guilt of my sin.
>
> Psalm 32:5

has been harboring. Explain that you are going to work on showing more kindness, gentleness, and grace, because you love him/her and you love God.

Do I ever get angry or grouchy with you?
How do I act when I'm angry?
How do you feel when I act that way?
What do you wish I would do instead?
What kinds of things do you think make me angry?
Do I ever make you angry? How?
Do I ever hurt your feelings?
Tell me about a time that I hurt your feelings.
Do you know that I love you, even when I'm grouchy?
When do you really feel like I love you? (Or, what kinds of things do I do that make you feel loved?)

Just for fun, download and print "What Does Mom Look Like?" from my website, beckykopitzke.com/crankymomfix. This fun worksheet, which is also in the Tools and Resources section in the back of this book, invites young kids to draw Mom's facial expressions when she's grumpy, happy, tired, etc.

Apologize in advance. I often take honesty a step further by acknowledging I'm on the brink of messing up—and apologizing while I'm still in possession of my sanity. Such as, "Sweetie, I'm sorry if I seem a little off today. I'm struggling with a headache and lots of deadlines on my desk. That's not your problem; it's mine. Will you please have extra grace for me?"

Allowing our kids to realize we're human is not bad parenting; it's healthy and wise. They need to know they can turn to Jesus when they're weary and weak. What better way to teach them than by example? A little vulnerability on Mom's part—as long as it's authentic and not intended to manipulate—can create a powerful lesson in God's mercy and strength.

> Come to me, all you who are weary and burdened, and I will give you rest.
>
> Matthew 11:28

Take a break. Sometimes escape is the best reaction to a trigger. If possible, walk away. Take a shower. Stuff your face in a pillow. Lock yourself in the bathroom for a few minutes if you have to, whatever it takes—just get the heck out of there before your tongue causes damage.

This can be tricky when kids are small and need your constant supervision. Even just a few seconds of deep breathing and squeezing your eyes shut can subdue the Momster enough to retract her claws and stop pouncing. We'll work on more spiritual responses in upcoming chapters, but for now, keep this one in your back pocket at all times. For real. I've done it a hundred times in the heat of a trigger. It works.

> Do not set foot on the path of the wicked or walk in the way of evildoers. Avoid it, do not travel on it; turn from it and go on your way.
>
> Proverbs 4:14–15

Ask for forgiveness. Finally, sweet mom friend, if you do blow it— as many loving moms before you have and will do again—say you're sorry. Humble yourself, own up to your mistakes, and ask God and your child for forgiveness. My children have so often reflected the face of God in their unquestioning willingness to forgive my infractions and move on. Perhaps if we want to know how to love our families well and without limits, we ought to take a lesson from our kids.

> Be kind and compassionate to one another, forgiving each other, just as in Christ God forgave you.
>
> Ephesians 4:32

 *Let's Dig In!*

1. Review your daily triggers assessment ("What Are My Triggers?"). Do you notice any recurring issues or triggers you weren't aware of before? How did this exercise help you pinpoint the deeper root of your crankiness? Continue using the assessment tool for as long as necessary until you become so familiar with your triggers that you're able to predict—and preempt—potential outbursts.

2. Do you think God cares how you handle your triggers? Why or why not? For insight, see Mark 14:38; James 1:12; Hebrews 4:15–16; James 1:2–4; and 1 Thessalonians 5:22.

3. Read 1 Corinthians 10:13. According to this verse, are our triggers unique? Not at all. Most of the temptations we face—those triggers that beckon us to get cranky—are actually quite common. God knew they would be an issue for us, and He also provides a way out. How can recognizing your triggers place you at an advantage in your quest to become a kinder, gentler mom? In what ways does God "not let you be tempted beyond what you can bear"? See 1 John 4:4; James 1:5; Matthew 4:1–11; 1 Thessalonians 5:23–24; and Ephesians 3:20.

4. Read Galatians 5:22–23. What qualities does the Spirit give us? Which of these do you feel are challenged when you face certain triggers? Here's the good news: If you've surrendered your life to Jesus, then the Holy Spirit dwells in you. That means you have access to those qualities or "fruit" of the Spirit listed in Galatians. They already live within you. It's just a matter of discovering how to wield them well.

5. Read 1 Corinthians 13:1–7. On the next page, write your name in the blanks.

_____ is patient, _____ is kind. _____ does not envy, _____ does not boast, _____ is not proud. _____ does not dishonor others, _____ is not self-seeking, _____ is not easily angered, _____ keeps no record of wrongs. _____ does not delight in evil but rejoices with the truth. _____ always protects, always trusts, always hopes, always perseveres.

Can you recite the above passage with confidence, using your own name as the subject? Why or why not? Which of these areas present the greatest challenge for you?

Patience	Dishonoring others
Kindness	Self-seeking/selfishness
Envy	Easily angered
Boastfulness	Keeping record of wrongs (unforgiveness/holding grudges)
Pride	Delighting in evil (falling prey to temptation)

6. First Corinthians 13:7 says love "always protects." Other translations say "love bears all things." The Greek word for *bears* here is *stegei* or *stegó*, which means to cover closely, as if to keep water out.[1] So essentially love is like a roof over our heads. It keeps us safe, dry, and protected from the elements. Are you such a safe place for your children? Are you protecting them from harsh weather, or are you sometimes causing the tornado? Pray for God to open your eyes and heart to what we're going to be exploring in the chapters ahead so you can begin making a habit of protecting your children from your own crankiness.

7. Also in verse 7, we read that love "always perseveres." The New Living Translation says it "endures through every circumstance." Be encouraged! It is possible to overcome crankiness even in the midst of circumstantial triggers. Remember why and how we are capable of loving in the first place. "We love because he first loved us" (1 John 4:19). God gives us

the power to love other people. Therefore, ask Him to help you better understand His love for you, so you can overflow that kind of abundant, unconditional love onto your family. For further study on the topic of God's amazing love, see Ephesians 3:16–19; Psalm 86:15; Zephaniah 3:17; Romans 8:37–39; John 3:16; Romans 5:8; and 1 John 4:9–11.

8. Read Hebrews 5:2. In the context surrounding this verse, Jesus is described as a high priest. A high priest in Jewish history was appointed. He couldn't just choose the job; God chose him.

In a way, parenting is similar to being a high priest. Why? Only God creates children, and only He—the Sovereign over everything and everyone—decides which children will be assigned to your family, whether by birth or adoption. In that sense, motherhood is a high and holy calling. And what does Hebrews 5 say about the role of high priest? "He [dare I say *she*] is able to deal gently with those who are ignorant and are going astray, since he himself is subject to weakness" (Hebrews 5:2, brackets mine).

Moms, we are able—through God's strength and wisdom—to deal gently with our children, who are often ignorant or mischievous simply because they are kids. And we do this not in spite of our weakness, but because of it. Our own failings should make us more sympathetic and sensitive to our children.

> May the God who gives endurance and encouragement
> give you the same attitude of mind toward each other that
> Christ Jesus had, so that with one mind and one voice you
> may glorify the God and Father of our Lord Jesus Christ.
> Accept one another, then, just as Christ accepted you, in
> order to bring praise to God.
>
> Romans 15:5–7

Therefore, pray that God would instill encouragement as your default response to your kids, even in frustrating situations.

3

Don't Snap. Do This Instead.

On a hot summer day in the final weeks of pregnancy, my friend Megan sat in her backyard supervising the kiddie pool. Her sons, ages four and two, had been bickering all morning and began fighting over their monstrous inflatable shark, which was bigger than the pool.

"My four-year-old earned a time-out for pushing his brother and was sitting beside me," Megan said. "I was hot, frustrated, a hundred weeks pregnant, and mad at myself for planting my son next to me for his time-out—I mean seriously, am I being punished, too? For four minutes straight, he did nothing but whine about the shark."

So she lost it.

"I'm going to stab that shark and throw it in the trash if you don't knock it off!"

Her son's jaw dropped, his eyes grew widely terrified, and he sat speechless for a few seconds. Then he replied, "If you do that, I'm going to punch you in the head."

Uh—not exactly the kind of family harmony we dream of when we imagine lazy summers by the pool, eh? But scenes like this one play out day after day in thousands of families across the world, in some form or fashion. Child acts naughty, Mom blows her top, child reacts—and why wouldn't he, considering Mom just demonstrated anger by example.

Hey, I've done it more times than I can count. If you have, too, then you're reading the right book. Welcome to the no-judgment zone.

"I was so shocked and had to hold back laughter because my son's response was so unexpected," Megan told me. She immediately regretted threatening to stab the shark and asked her son for forgiveness. They also talked about why we shouldn't punch people in the head. "It's those moments that turn out to be the sweetest, even in spite of our mess-ups, because they open up conversations about the gospel and how we are all in need of Jesus!"

Be encouraged. Our mistakes are often beautifully redeemed, and such God-soaked resolutions are the consolation prize of many mom fails. However, I do want us to consider this: How might a different response in the first place have prevented the need for repair? Do we have a choice that does not involve snapping and regret? Of course we do. Remember from chapter 1, the devil is not in charge of you. "Cranky" is not our only option.

Let's explore four strategies that can serve as trusty alternatives to losing your momma cool. I've used them, I've memorized them, and I've stocked them in my heart's arsenal of weapons against the Momster. I hope you will, too.

1. The Quick Switch

In my first book, *The SuperMom Myth*, I introduced a concept that has saved my tail many times, and it's one I encourage you to embrace from this day forward. I call it the Quick Switch.

The idea is simple really. Whenever a negative thought pops into your head, quickly "switch it" or replace it with an affirming thought or Bible verse. For example:

—— Quick Switch Cheat Sheet ——

Here are some verses that work great for the Quick Switch. Choose a few that are meaningful to you, and commit them to memory. Then use them every chance you get! God's Word is empowering!

- "The wise woman builds her house, but with her own hands the foolish one tears hers down" (Proverbs 14:1).
- "[Parents], do not embitter your children, or they will become discouraged" (Colossians 3:21).
- "Do not let any unwholesome talk come out of your mouths, but only what is helpful for building others up according to their needs, that it may benefit those who listen" (Ephesians 4:29).
- "A person's wisdom yields patience; it is to one's glory to overlook an offense" (Proverbs 19:11).
- "The words of the reckless pierce like swords, but the tongue of the wise brings healing" (Proverbs 12:18).
- "A gentle answer turns away wrath, but a harsh word stirs up anger" (Proverbs 15:1).
- "Set a guard over my mouth, Lord; keep watch over the door of my lips" (Psalm 141:3).
- "Love is patient, love is kind" (1 Corinthians 13:4).

For each member of your family, write a list of affirming truths that you can use when you need to pull out the Quick Switch.

Me: *She did not seriously just spill that nail polish on the new carpet. I'm going to scream.*

Quick Switch: "Set a guard over my mouth, Lord; keep watch over the door of my lips" (Psalm 141:3).

[Example] Name: My Husband

1. He is loyal.
2. He is wonderfully involved with the kids.
3. He's a responsible provider.

Name: _____
1. _____
2. _____
3. _____

Name: _____
1. _____
2. _____
3. _____

Name: _____
1. _____
2. _____
3. _____

Name: _____
1. _____
2. _____
3. _____

No, I did not plan on googling "how to get blue nail polish out of beige carpet" today, but what's done is done and we can't take it back. Haven't I made mistakes before, too? Showing grace to my daughter in this moment will demonstrate Christ-like character—shockingly merciful and calm—whereas lashing out will crumble my witness in two seconds flat.

Me: *I really want to harp on my husband right now for neglecting to put my car keys on the hook where the car keys live. How am I supposed to drive if he hides my keys?*

Quick Switch: "The wise woman builds her house, but with her own hands the foolish one tears hers down" (Proverbs 14:1).

Nagging tears down. My husband does a thousand things well, all of which far overshadow this momentary annoyance. He is loyal. He adores our kids. He knows how to fix the sink. And so much more. Therefore, if I want to build my house, I'll focus on his many positives instead of this one little irk. Ask nicely for the car keys, woman. You'll be glad you did.

Me: *I've told my daughters three times to stop whispering and turn the lights out. If I hear one more peep from their room, I'm barging in with threats of grounding—to separate rooms. For a week! A month! Until the day they move to college, heaven help us all!!!*

Quick Switch: "A gentle answer turns away wrath, but a harsh word stirs up anger" (Proverbs 15:1).

My daughters have a sweet relationship. They could be fighting instead of giggling—but they're not. They're telling stories, cracking jokes, building memories. Yes, I'm tired (trigger!) and they are ignoring my instructions (trigger!), but I will address their disobedience gently, without turning into a witch.

How? Ah—that's what we're going to talk about next. But first, don't skip this step. A simmering pot is far less likely to explode than a pressure cooker. In the heat of the moment, use the Quick Switch to deflate your anger *before* you react. Not only will it prevent blowups, it'll also fuel your heart and soul with Scripture—the best defense against temptation.

> We demolish arguments and every pretension that sets itself up against the knowledge of God, and we take captive every thought to make it obedient to Christ.
>
> 2 Corinthians 10:5

2. Speak Love, Not War

Two people examine the same cup of coffee. One says it's half full; the other says it's half empty. Which one is right? Well, they both are. But one of them is certainly more depressing.

> The soothing tongue is a tree of life, but a perverse tongue crushes the spirit.
>
> Proverbs 15:4

When we speak to our kids, we have a choice. We can speak life or we can speak death. One is encouraging, hope-filled, and kind. The other is cutting and condemning. Which way we go depends largely on where our hearts steer us, because "a good person produces good things from the treasury of a good heart, and an evil person produces evil things from the treasury of an evil heart. What you say flows from what is in your heart" (Luke 6:45, NLT).

So let me ask. What's in your heart? How does your heart perceive your children, your husband, your household? How we view a situation will determine how we speak over it. And as moms we must decide—are we at war with our kids, or aiming to live in peace?

Whether we realize it or not, when conflicts arise, many of us view our homes as enemy territory. It's us against them! Children vs. parents, husband vs. wife! We forget we are on the same team, so we shoot words like arrows meant to defend and disarm. Not consciously, perhaps, and certainly not all the time. I know very few women who would actually claim their children are the enemy, or vice versa. Yet in subtle ways, we allow this mentality to taint our conversations.

Megan, for example—she was hot and exhausted (trigger!), and her children were defying the rules (trigger!); therefore, she saw their backyard as a battleground and let an arrow fly.

My friend Carolyn got tired of her four-year-old begging for an "ultimate cream pie" just ten minutes before supper was due to fill his belly. She said no; he asked again. She said "No, not until after dinner," and he screamed, "I *said* I want an ultimate cream pie!!" Carolyn watched her son flailing on the kitchen floor, grabbed an *oatmeal* cream pie from the cupboard, and tossed it at him like the closing pitch of a baseball game. "Fine!" she yelled. "But I'm still the parent!"

Every single morning I personally endure the mother-classic battle of wills called *getting to school on time*. I scramble to pack the lunches, brush the hair, find the missing socks, *and* take my own shower on a good day—please, Lord—yet my children have no sympathy. They demand more waffles, whine that their pants are too scratchy, or choose this of all moments to melt into a puddle of tears, but the clock keeps ticking and I'm obliged to remind them, "Get your shoes on NOW or I'm leaving without you and you can walk five miles to school in the POURING RAIN, aaaaaaaaargghhhhh!"

Is there a better way to say that? You bet there is. But in the heat of frustration and triggers galore, I sometimes allow the devil to suggest my children are against me. Therefore, my words go to war. Yours, too?

Here are three steps to take when we're tempted to speak harshly.

1. *Tell Satan to take a flying leap.* Your home is a sanctuary, allied territory, a place of peace, and that's a fact. Don't allow the devil to convince you otherwise.
2. *Utilize the Quick Switch.* Deflate with a Scripture recall, such as, "Gracious words are a honeycomb, sweet to the soul and healing to the bones" (Proverbs 16:24). Fill your heart with truth so you can *speak truth*!
3. *Choose "cup half full" words.* Circumstances may not change—the kids are bickering, whining, and begging, and we're all running late, yes, indeed—but "put your #$@&%* shoes on!" could just as effectively come out as, "Hey, remember your shoes? Put them on please, and thank you."

Is this easy? Absolutely not. We will all slip up from time to time, but the more we practice, and the closer we tune our hearts to God and His Word, the more those "honeycomb" words will flow by default. And when they do, count it a victory, dear one—of eternal proportions.

3. Get Goofy

When our triggers are tripped, the easy response is to blow. It's much harder to do the right thing and practice self-control. But does self-control always mean we have to stuff our vexation? Or can we let it come out another way—a more effective, harmonious, merrily-we-roll-along sort of way?

> Fools give full vent to their rage, but the wise bring calm in the end.
>
> Proverbs 29:11

— Gentle Answers Work Sheet —

Read these common cranky-mom statements, then write a kinder way of saying the same thing. Add your own frequent cranky mom-isms and practice "speaking love, not war" instead.

1. [Example] "Hurry up! We're going to be late!"

   [Gentle Translation] "Let's have a race! See if you can get your jacket on faster than I can."

2. "Turn off the TV now, this instant!"

   _____

   _____

3. "Life isn't fair. Get over it."

   _____

   _____

4. "What in the world is WRONG with you?"

   _____

   _____

5. _____

   _____

   _____

6. _____

   _____

   _____

7. _____

   _____

   _____

8. _____

   _____

   _____

One of the smartest ways to dispel frustration in the house—especially around children—is by acting spontaneously goofy. Try these silly strategies for blowing off steam without blowing up at your kids.

1. *Sing a song.* No, really. When you're feeling the urge to purge your vocal cords, try belting out a tune instead of hollering. "Shout to the Lord" works great, in my personal experience. Or perhaps you're a count-to-ten kind of parent, in which case I recommend the *Sesame Street* version. (One-two-three-FOUR-five—six-seven-eight-NINE-ten—eleven TWE-E-E-E-E-E-ELVE!) Not only can this strategy help loosen your cranky pants, but the kids will look at you like you've lost your mind and maybe even start to laugh. So there you have it. Tension broken; problem solved.

2. *Tell a joke.* Speaking of laughing, why not flip your anger on its head and distract the kids with a few kicks and giggles? Knock-knock jokes work great for this. (Shout "knock-knock!" a few times and see if that doesn't make you feel better.)

3. *Dance.* It's purely scientific. When your kids irk you, your body generates a surge of cortisol. We think we want to release these "fight or flight" hormones by screaming, but that only hurts everyone more in the end. So instead, try burning off your frustration with exercise—namely, dancing! A sudden burst of the cabbage patch will confuse your kids long enough to forget what they were whining about in the first place, and it'll help you switch mental gears, too. Best-case scenario, the kids will join in, and soon you'll all be celebrating an impromptu dance party in the kitchen.

4. Ask Permission (Stop, Pray, Obey)

My younger daughter used to suck her thumb. At first, when she was a bitty thing, my husband and I thought it was sweet. She was colicky

Favorite Family
Knock-Knock Jokes

Knock knock.
Who's there?
Ice cream soda.
Ice cream soda who?
Ice cream soda people can hear me!

Knock knock.
Who's there?
Hawaii.
Hawaii who?
I'm doing fine, thanks. Hawaii doing?

Knock knock.
Who's there?
Ash.
Ash who?
Gesundheit!

Knock knock.
Who's there?
Yoda lady.
Yoda lady who?
Wow, I didn't know you could yodel!

Knock knock.
Who's there?
Wa.
Wa who?
What are you so excited about?

Knock knock.
Who's there?
Cash.
Cash who?
No thanks, I prefer peanuts.

Knock knock.
Who's there?
Juicy.
Juicy who?
Juicy my car keys anywhere?

Knock knock.
Who's there?
Alda.
Alda who?
That's Alda jokes I've got. Good-bye!

anyhow, so we appreciated the thumb's magical soothing properties. But then as our girl grew toward preschool, we stared down a fortune in orthodontist bills and decided the thumb had to go (so to speak).

My daughter knew this. And she didn't like it.

"Momma, can I suck my thumb? I'm kind of tired." She looped an arm around my leg, looked up at my face, and batted her puppy eyes. I blew a deep sigh because back then I'd hear this exact request about a dozen times a day.

See, rather than sneaking around or openly defying my expectations, my daughter simply asked permission to bend the rules. And because my softie mom heart feared that giving up the thumb was like asking a smoker to quit cold turkey, I gave her a transition period, like a nicotine patch, in which she was allowed to suck her thumb only when she went to sleep.

Therefore, the question was always, "MommacanIsuckmythumbImkindoftired."

When I said no, she threw fits. Naturally.

When I caved and said *okay fine*—usually in moments of frustration for the sake of my own sanity—she would smile and curl into a ball on the sofa, quiet and content. Temporarily. Because even she knew she was delaying the inevitable.

That thumb was trouble. The longer we let it go on, the more damage it would do. We all realized this. It was just so hard to break the habit.

Sound familiar?

I wonder, though. What if, like my daughter did, we stopped to ask permission—from God? Anytime we're tempted to do something He disapproves, to engage in old, cranky habits—what if we turned our eyes to the sky and begged?

God, can I snap at my husband? I'm kind of tired.

Lord, can I hurry my kids and ignore their hearts? I'm kind of on a schedule here.

Heavenly Father, would you mind if I nagged incessantly about that thing I cannot change? I know you've got it covered, but right now I'm kind of freaking out. You understand.

What do you think God would say?

Oh, there are plenty of Bible verses granting us clear direction on certain behaviors and attitudes. But I started responding to my daughter with one simple question of my own: "What do you think?" And I wonder if God would do the same.

"I have the right to do anything," you say—but not everything is beneficial. "I have the right to do anything"—but not everything is constructive. No one should seek their own good, but the good of others.

1 Corinthians 10:23–24

God gave us free will. Knowing right from wrong and lost from found is an important first step in using that free will wisely. But what if we went beyond the "rules" and considered how our choices affect not just us but other people? How would that change our decisions?

Yes, I might be tired. But that's not my husband's fault. He doesn't deserve my snappishness.

I'm busy and distracted again, yep. But it's not all about me. I owe my kids my presence.

Here I am, buried in my fears and what-ifs. But you, Lord, are working within them and through them and above them for some purpose I cannot see. I know it's the right choice to trust you. Will you help me?

"Momma, can I suck my thumb? I'm kind of tired." My daughter lifted her hand to her mouth and waited for my reply.

"What do you think, sweetheart?"

She stood motionless, with her thumb suspended in midair, and stared at me for a good three seconds.

"I'm gonna do it. Thanks, Mom!" And off she ran to the couch, where she curled into her usual snuggle ball and sucked away.

What was I saying about free will? It took my daughter another couple years to stop sucking her thumb—and then only when her orthodontist told her to and we were already three thousand dollars in the hole. But hey, I'm forty-some years old and I still haven't completely figured out how to make the right choices at the right time. Have you?

Ask God for permission. Now, that's a clever place to start. Because, unlike my daughter's thumb habit, stopping to talk with the Lord Almighty before making a dumb move could very well prevent the dumb move from happening. Who wants to disappoint God, right?

Stop. Pray. Obey.

What a simple formula for Christian living. It just might change the world.

 *Let's Dig In!*

1. Read Colossians 3:21. What should we *not* do to our children? The Greek reference for *embitter* also means "provoke" or "exasperate."[1] What do you picture when you think of provoking, exasperating, or embittering your children? How can each of the following strategies we've learned help to prevent this?

   • Quick Switch
   • Speak love, not war
   • Get goofy
   • Stop, pray, obey

2. The second part of Colossians 3:21 tells us what will happen if we continue to embitter our children. They will become discouraged. That, once again, is the opposite of "building your house" (Proverbs 14:1). Read 1 Thessalonians 5:11 and Hebrews 3:13. The Greek word for *encourage* in these verses, *parakaleite*, means "to comfort, teach, instruct, and build up."[2] Isn't that exactly what we're called to do as moms? What are some ways you can encourage your children today?

3. Read Ephesians 4:29. What do you think qualifies as unwholesome talk? Make a list. How many of these types of talk do you engage in? (For example: yelling, swearing, gossiping, using the Lord's name in vain.) Did you notice this verse mentions once again the importance of building others up? It's a Proverbs 14:1 theme! In what ways can your words build up your children? In what ways can they tear them down?

4. The Greek word for *unwholesome* in Ephesians 4:29 is *sapros*, meaning "corrupted, unfit for use, rotten, or putrefied."[3] Yuck! Next time you yell, snap, or belittle your children, imagine a load of smelly, gaseous slime spewing out of your mouth. I call this verbal vomit. Once it shoots out, it splatters everywhere, and it's super hard to clean up. It clings to hurt feelings and creates nasty stains.

   But there's good news! God offers preventive therapy. Read Psalm 141:3. Aren't you relieved to know even the psalmist recognized he had a problem with verbal vomit? Be encouraged: your struggle is nothing new and you are not alone. Yet God does want to help you control it. Pray regularly for God to "set a guard over your mouth" to keep that putrid stuff from seeping out.

5. Read Proverbs 19:11. The wiser we get, the more patience we'll have. Why do you think that is? Remember Let's Dig In! question 4 of chapter 1: The source of our wisdom is God and His Word. The more we study Scripture and spend time with the Lord in prayer, the closer we'll draw to Him, and the wiser, more patient we'll become.

   Remember in this chapter we discussed Luke 6:45, which tells us, "What you say flows from what is in your heart" (NLT). Now see also Psalm 119:11. One of my pastors once called this the process of becoming God-soaked. When we understand God's will and memorize His Word, we become like a sponge filled with God's truth. Then anytime we get "squeezed" or tempted, God's truth comes out. That's the concept behind the Quick Switch!

6. What does it mean to overlook an offense (Proverbs 19:11)? Before we take issue with every annoying thing our children (and husbands) do, let's ask ourselves—is this worth a fight? A kind and loving mother is wise to pick her battles. Constantly nagging our family for minor infractions can create an environment in which they feel unaccepted or fearful. And that is exactly what Colossians 3:21 warns against.

   The original Hebrew word used in Proverbs 19:11 for *overlook* is *abar*, which means "to pass over."[4] Throughout the Old Testament, this term is used to describe travel, such as passing through a territory, over a border, or across a river. Next time you're tempted to blow up at your kids, imagine yourself traveling through your anger and crossing to a safety zone on the other side.

7. Read Proverbs 12:18. I like the simplicity of the New Living Translation: "Some people make cutting remarks, but the words of the wise bring healing." Once again, we're talking about the wise woman. Does she cut her family to shreds with her mouth? Nope. Just the opposite. Her words heal.

   We are more susceptible to making cutting remarks when we're battling our triggers. For example, when I'm tired I'm much more likely to speak thoughtless or snappish words. Same goes for when I'm running late, distracted, or suffering from a headache. Review your "What Are My Triggers?" sheet. Can you see a connection between those triggers and your tendency to make cutting remarks?

8. Read Psalm 19:14. God doesn't just hear our words. He knows our hearts. Our desire should be to move beyond the surface (i.e., what comes out of our mouths) and repair the motives behind our words. How? Begin by praying Psalm 19:14 and Psalm 51:10 daily. Remember James 1:5 from Let's Dig In! question 4, chapter 1: Whenever we lack wisdom, we

can ask God for it and He will grant it generously, without scolding us for needing the wisdom in the first place. So ask boldly.

Let us then approach God's throne of grace with confidence, so that we may receive mercy and find grace to help us in our time of need.

Hebrews 4:16

4

When You Reach Your Limit

I used to have this little habit of throwing things when I got mad. Hairbrushes, kitchen towels, once an entire bottle of sunscreen—which cracked open midair and splattered all over the carpet *and* my brand-new canvas purse. I never did get the stain out.

Booger.

So imagine how relieved I felt when I discovered I wasn't the only mom who does this.

"My son was whining and badgering his little brother relentlessly, so I sent him to his room to calm down," my friend Karyn told me. Instead of taking a breather, her son got angrier and refused to stay in his room. "Each time he came out, I told him to go back, until my own behavior boiled over and became just as ridiculous as his—and I threw a shoe at him."

Will all the exasperated mommas please raise their hands.

However, Karyn's little fit backfired. "I'm not a very good aim," she said. "The shoe bounced off my son's door and hit my favorite statue of a girl reading a book—which I've always liked to think of as a Bible—and it broke her head off. Oh, and this all occurred in front of my son's best friend, who witnessed everything. Just call me Mother of the Year."

Uh-huh. But if that's what it takes to earn the title, Karyn would have some competition, because there are a whole lot of us frustrated mothers out there who qualify.

And we kind of hate ourselves for it, don't we?

It's so easy to allow our negative emotions to control our behavior. What's hard is the aftermath—when we inevitably bear the burden of guilt and remorse over whatever we said or did that we wish we hadn't. That's when it's critical to remember God's grace.

> For everyone has sinned; we all fall short of God's glorious standard. Yet God, in his grace, freely makes us right in his sight. He did this through Christ Jesus when he freed us from the penalty for our sins.
>
> Romans 3:23–24 NLT

Let's explore several tips for handling our parenting blunders in a God-honoring way. Then, before this chapter is through, we're going to discover how to pin that mom guilt to the cross and leave it there.

What If I Blow It?

My mom mess-ups often happen in the morning, just minutes before we're due to leave for school. Something trips my Momster alarm—lost homework, laziness, eye-rolling attitudes—so I bark. And growl and snap and bare my teeth. And a beautiful young person melts in a puddle of tears just when she's supposed to be zipping her backpack and putting on her (missing) shoes.

Then I collapse into a puddle of my own variety—regret.

Ugh. Mom fails. We've all had them. And we'll inevitably have them again, maybe tomorrow, or today. These shameful grown-up tantrums, sparked by any number of catalysts—disobedience, dawdling, our own touchy exhaustion, you name it—are sadly common among the mother set. But that doesn't make them any easier to bear.

Maybe you can relate to my friend Lisa's story.

"There's nothing I love more than an early morning road trip for an all-day basketball tournament an hour away," she told me, not without a spoonful of sarcasm. "Seriously, I do love cheering my player on, but with four kids it's a big divide-and-conquer endeavor between my husband and me. These trips are not a small deal."

So after forty-five minutes of driving, Lisa's son caught her attention in the rearview mirror and announced with a smirk, "I think I might have forgotten my bag at home." Lisa returned the smirk and assured him how *not* funny it would be if that turned out to be true.

"I saw tears welling in his eyes and a look of guilt wash over his face, but they weren't enough to prevent some awful things from spewing out of my mouth," Lisa confessed.

"You had only one thing to remember—a bag, that was it!"

"We already pay a boatload of money for these tournaments, and now we have to buy new shoes? Are you kidding me?!"

"I planned our trip just right so you'd be on time, and I don't have thirty minutes to spare for shoe shopping! You're going to be late! You're letting your whole team down!"

According to Lisa, that's the abbreviated, G-rated version.

When she shared this story with me, I have to admit Lisa's words pierced my heart because I had similarly drilled into my own daughter just a few days before. She'd been selected a month prior to participate in the school-wide geography bee and begged me to buy her the study guide, which I did. Then one morning (always in the morning, I'm telling you!) she sprang the news— *the geo bee is tomorrow!*—and she had hardly cracked open the book I paid for.

I berated her for wasting an opportunity, for neglecting to study, for not appreciating my generosity, and of course for playing on her iPod when she could've been examining her maps these past four weeks. Yes! It's the iPod's fault! Let's skirt the real issue and blame everything on that little source of all evil. As if it's not also my job to monitor screen time in the first place!

I mean, come on, people. Did I actually expect my ten-year-old to stick her nose in an atlas every night—and over Christmas break, for crying out loud? Talk about a mother's deluded perfectionism spilling over onto her offspring.

Both Lisa and I retracted our words and patched over the hurt. Her son made it to the game on time—with a new pair of shoes that even matched his uniform, praise God for small blessings. And my daughter and I threw a study party with pizza and M&Ms, during which I realized how impossible it actually is to prepare for the National Geographic GeoBee no matter how much she might have crammed. Then, you know what? That little stinker ended up tying for third place anyway—the youngest of the final four contestants by two grades.

God is funny.

But our behavior is not.

"A few blisters, some extensive apologies on both our ends, and I'm confident the mistake will not reoccur," Lisa said. "However, the mom regret is seared in my memory."

How is an otherwise sane and loving woman supposed to handle the aftermath of her weakest, ugliest moments? I don't know all the answers. If I did, I wouldn't need a clean-up plan to begin with—nor a stash of apology M&Ms, which I now keep on hand daily.

But from experience I can tell you there are wiser ways to approach our mistakes. Through trial and error—and a lot of time spent with God—I've discovered some hard-fought advice on how to manage those wretched mom fails. I hope they will bless you and your victims alike.

How to Repair a Nasty Mom Fail

First, humble yourself—before the Lord and your children. Ask God to reveal your part in the mess, then own it, and back down. I call this the deflating moment. When I get all puffed up with anger and pride, and steam blows out my nose and nasty words shoot out of my mouth, I'm like a rocket at countdown time. There comes a moment when we must release the anger and free-fall back into God's waiting arms. Exhale. Crumple like a landed parachute and welcome your kids back into your safe space.

Acknowledge your mistake—and by this I mean talk about it. Tell your kids you messed up and you know it. Be vulnerable. If your kids are old enough to understand, explain to them how your own issues got in the way of you responding well. This doesn't dilute your authority; it reveals your dependence on Jesus, which is one of the best lessons we can teach our kids by example. If we skip this step, the conflict can remain hanging in the air like a storm cloud. Don't let them live in fear. It's up to us to dispel it.

Ask for forgiveness—and be amazed at how easily they give it. My kids often show me the untainted love of Christ in their pure willingness to forgive and move on. Yes, I may wish I hadn't blown up in the first place, but heartfelt apologies can redeem the situation by showing our children how much we, too, depend on God's mercy—and then giving them a chance to share it.

Hold your child responsible—for her part in the blow-up. Mom fails are often sparked by a child's behavior or decision, like we saw with Karyn, Lisa, and me. Just because we didn't handle our situations well doesn't mean the trigger wasn't a valid problem.

Karyn's son should have stayed in his room. Lisa's son should have remembered his gym bag. My daughter should have put a little more effort into preparing for the GeoBee. These are real mistakes on the child's part—or better yet, call them opportunities for improvement.

Therefore, after we moms admit we didn't react well and have asked our children for forgiveness, we still need to address what our kids might have done differently. Not in a way that suggests they were to blame for *our* behavior, but rather as a calm and intentional parent who's more interested in guiding than condemning.

Brainstorm solutions together—Empower your child to help prevent these nasty blow-ups in the future by inviting him to be part of the solution. Ask, "How can I help you . . ." (get ready for school on time, remember to finish your homework, say no to drugs—whatever the case may be)? Reestablish your relationship as a team. You're on the same side.

And finally, remind your children they are loved—unconditionally. Your love for them is not dependent on their behavior. Your acceptance does not hinge on their decisions. As moms, we're called to love our kids as Jesus loves—especially when they sin. Because that's what God is all about.

> While we were still sinners, Christ died for us.
>
> Romans 5:8

I wish I could guarantee I'll never need to use these six tips again myself, but I know I will. It's part of being human in a fallen, selfish world. Yet, thankfully, the same promise Jesus gives our kids He also gives to us: grace, mercy, and forgiveness—the pillars of His love.

> Because of the Lord's great love we are not consumed, for his compassions never fail. They are new every morning; great is your faithfulness.
>
> Lamentations 3:22–23

Mom, Mom, Mom, Mom, Mom, Mom, Mom

I love my children to the core of my soul. And you know what else I love?

Silence.

Funny, isn't it? Because we all know those two things cannot exist simultaneously unless someone is either sleeping or drugged.

Mom, can you help me?

Mom, look at this.

Mom, I can't reach the crackers!

Mom, guess what Sam told me at school yesterday.

Mom, I need more orange juice.

Mom, can I sit on your lap?

Mom, Mom, Mom, Mom, Mom, Mom, Mom!

Aaaack!!! Can everybody leave me alone for one tiny precious minute, for the love of peace on earth, I'm begging you, PLEEEEASE!!!

Whenever I get buzzed to the edge of my nerves from all the "Mom, Mom, Mom, Mom, Mom, Mom, Mom" demands, I remind myself of three very important things. I want you to believe them, too.

1. It's okay to feel this way. Getting frustrated with parenting doesn't mean you love your kids any less. It doesn't mean you're weak or missing some magic maternal nurturing gene. For crying out loud, we're human. My brain is not wired for constant input, is yours? So the last thing we need in those moments of burnout is to add guilt to the emotional pile. Give yourself permission to be real.

There is now no condemnation for those who are in Christ Jesus.

Romans 8:1

2. It's not the kids' fault. They love you. They need you. They don't care if their own legs can transport them to the cupboard to get the bag of pretzels all by their lonesome, because YOU are the center of their world and it's natural to lean on Mom. Yes, we need to train them to do things for themselves, but that's a different conversation. What we're talking about here is our emotional capacity for being smothered. In the moment, do you snap at your kiddos as if it's all their fault that Mom is losing her flapping mind? Then consider this. Your child didn't ask to be your kid. That was kind of your doing. Or, more accurately, God's. Do we really want to go down that road?

> Your hands made me and formed me; give me understanding to learn your commands.
>
> Psalm 119:73

Nothing but our own sin nature is to blame for our frustrations. So beware of the temptation to view your children as the enemy. They're on your team.

3. This noise is a gift. In the heat of a mother meltdown, the last thing we feel like doing is counting our blessings. But I've got to tell you—I've walked alongside some dear friends recently who have lost their children too young. These beautiful women would do anything to hear their kids say "Mom" one more time. Or to ask them for a glass of water or a Snickers bar in the checkout lane.

Why do I deserve to have my babies here with me, watching YouTube videos in the living room, begging for buttered noodles while they scatter paper crafts across the floor, when other God-fearing women are grieving in too-quiet houses still filled with the presence of a precious child lost?

I don't. No one does. Not a single one of us deserves the blessings we have and too often take for granted. They're a gift from God. He gives them freely and, I hate to say it but it's true, He can freely take them away. So when I get all crabby-pants and stuck on my own entitlement to silence and freedom, just for a split second—I don't dwell there—I remind myself that I might get what I ask for. Heaven forbid.

> Children are a heritage from the Lord, offspring a reward from him.
>
> Psalm 127:3

So then, sweet mom friend. If you're having one of those Mom-Mom-Mom days, wishing you could fly away just for a few minutes or hours or weeks, by all means, lock yourself in a room if you can while the kids eat ridiculous servings of whatever keeps their mouths occupied. But please—please—remember this:

It's okay to have limits.

It's nobody's fault.

And even the crazy, I've-had-it-up-to-here moments are ordained by God. He is so good to us. And He loves us just the way we are—frazzled, imperfect, and tired.

Praise the Lord.

Let's Dig In!

1. Read Hebrews 4:13; Proverbs 15:3; and Psalm 139:1–5. What do these verses tell us about God? How do you feel about the realization that God is always with you and always watching? Does this make you feel comforted? Fearful? Guilty?

2. Read Hebrews 4:16. What does God offer to us when we need it most? Next, recall Romans 8:1. Our God is a merciful God. If you are a follower of Jesus, then God does not condemn you for your mistakes. He may, however, *convict* you or point out an opportunity to improve your character. This is not meant as punishment but rather an awakening— a chance to become aware of your sin and do something about it. Conviction is an *invitation* to draw closer to God. Welcome it—and He will welcome *you* with open arms.

3. Recall the six "mom fail" recovery steps we discussed in this chapter:
   - Humble yourself
   - Acknowledge your mistake

- Ask forgiveness
- Hold your child responsible
- Brainstorm solutions together
- Remind your children they are loved

Which of these is most difficult for you, and why? Which had you never considered before? Next time you face a mom fail, apply these steps and take note of the outcome. Journal or discuss the situation with a friend.

4. Why is humility an important ingredient in taming the Momster? See Proverbs 11:2. What does humility generate? Now read Colossians 3:12–14. God wants us to "wear" humility like a garment. What does that word picture say to you? What other positive qualities are we also commanded to "wear"? How can we apply these virtues to our relationship with our children?

5. Do you sometimes feel like you've reached your max capacity for input? Like the constant noise, requests, discipline, and demands of parenting are squeezing your nerves and draining your spirit? No human being is capable of consistent

Colossians 3:12–14

Memorize Colossians 3:12–14! Visit beckykopitzke.com/cranky momfix for a gallery wall printable of this passage, as well as a lock-screen version for your computer or mobile device.

Therefore, as God's chosen people, holy and dearly loved, clothe yourselves with compassion, kindness, humility, gentleness and patience. Bear with each other and forgive one another if any of you has a grievance against someone. Forgive as the Lord forgave you. And over all these virtues put on love, which binds them all together in perfect unity.

Colossians 3:12–14

overload. Even Jesus needed time to rest and pray. Throughout the Gospels, we read accounts of Jesus leaving the crowds and their endless needs in order to do what mattered even more than serving others: seeking God. For example, see Mark 1:35; Mark 6:31; Matthew 14:23; and Luke 6:12. Now read Genesis 2:2–3. Even God rested!

6. Do you feel guilty for needing a break? Don't. Seeking time to refuel your body and soul is not only normal but also healthy. See Matthew 11:28–29 and Psalm 127:2.

7. Read 1 Kings 19:1–8. Note Elijah's attitude in this passage. Sounds kind of familiar, doesn't it? He's fed up, weary, and wishing for all of his responsibilities to go away. He's running away from them actually. Have you ever wanted to fly away, too? So what does God do to Elijah? Does He reprimand him? Does He give him a lecture or remind him to pray harder? No. God sends an angel to feed Elijah and give him rest. Our physical and mental health needs are important to God. Why is it difficult to make self-care a priority in your life? What small changes can you begin making toward that end?

8. Read Psalm 51:6. The Amplified Bible translation says, "You desire truth in the innermost being." This means we don't need to hide our emotions from God. On the contrary, He wants us to be honest, vulnerable, and raw with Him. Are you willing to do that? The Lord is a safe place to reveal our flaws; after all, He already knows them better than we do. Therefore, whenever you're frustrated, angry, impatient, etc., acknowledge how you're feeling, and bring it to God. Spend some time in prayer confessing your struggles and asking God to fuel you with His wisdom, grace, and strength.

> Come to me, all you who are weary and burdened, and I will give you rest.
>
> Matthew 11:28

5

Self-Care—the New "S" Word

At age seven, my younger daughter was delightfully ignorant of swear words. She hadn't heard them, never said them, and didn't even know such language existed—until one day she came home from school with this story.

"Mom, Jackson said the 'S' word today."

I turned toward her with my eyebrows raised, looked square into her sweet face, and played all nonchalant. "He did? Well, that wasn't very nice." And then, because I figured this conversation was doomed from the start, I asked the leading question. "What did he say?"

"Well, we were playing a game at recess, and he got mad and said the game was, you know . . . *stupid*!"

"Stupid? He said—stupid? The 'S' word?"

"Yes, Mom!" Her eyes grew wide and she pushed her knuckles into her knees. "Don't keep saying it! You know it's a bad word!"

Oh, the innocence of children. I'll cling to it as long as I can.

As grown-ups, we might allow ourselves a few more liberties in language, yet most of us do and should avoid certain words as improper or ungodly. The trouble comes when we add words to the "naughty" list that God never intended to be there.

Like *self-care*.

What? You can't say that in a parenting book! We're mothers, for heaven's sake—we care for other people, not ourselves! Serve, give, sacrifice—these are the tenets of our job description!

Perhaps. But not at the expense of our bodies and souls.

In many Christian mom circles, *self-care* is the new "S" word. We avoid it for the sake of piety. We believe a truly loving mother will cast herself aside for the good of her children, and to some degree that is true. Motherhood is a selfless, demanding, heart-wrenching calling for which the rewards far outweigh the sacrifice.

But what happens when we allow ourselves to get so run down that we're useless to everyone around us—especially our children? Is that the work of a "good" Christian mom? I don't think so. Neither does God.

> Unless the Lord builds a house, the builders' work is useless. Unless the Lord protects a city, sentries do no good. It is senseless for you to work so hard from early morning until late at night, fearing you will starve to death; for God wants his loved ones to get their proper rest.
>
> Psalm 127:1–2 TLB

When we work, work, work and serve, serve, serve our families with no respect for our own need for "proper rest"—which means not only sleep or relaxation but also time spent with God—our efforts are futile. God must be in charge. Trouble is, many of us are too busy trying to do His job.

We are faulty human beings. We have limits. And like we just discussed in chapter 4, when we hit those limits, our moods suffer. Ironically, not taking care of ourselves can become the very root of our grouchiness and completely defeat the goal of motherly kindness. Therefore, self-care is not selfish. It's a critical component in our Cranky Mom Fix.

You Are Worth More than Your Children's Leftovers

We were in a rush, like usual. It was a typical school morning in our house—get the kids dressed, lunches packed, teeth brushed. "Grab those backpacks, everyone, and don't forget your sweater, your water bottle, your homework, your hugs!"

By the time my young people were safely squirreled away at desks across town and I returned home to a pile of their breakfast dishes, my own stomach grumbled.

Oh yeah. I should eat, too.

So I glanced at a plate of picked-over French toast and considered my options.

Spend twenty minutes making myself a fresh and nutritious breakfast—while I've got deadlines at my desk and an even bigger pile of laundry to sort and about a hundred emails to scan, tick-tock, tick-tock.

Or.

Eat my child's leftovers in thirty seconds, tops. So what if I'm sensitive to the gluten and the sugar gives me cramps and the entire plate is cold and congealed by now—but hey, it's sitting right in front of me and it'd be such a shame to waste it—and we all know busy women can't be picky, right?

Or can they?

> Haven't you yet learned that your body is the home of the Holy Spirit God gave you, and that he lives within you? Your own body does not belong to you. For God has bought you with a great price. So use every part of your body to give glory back to God because he owns it.
>
> 1 Corinthians 6:19–20 TLB

As moms buried in the daily grind, our well-being comes down to a choice: take care of ourselves, or don't. And I'm ashamed of how often I pick the wrong one. You, too?

French toast is just a symptom of a much deeper issue. Those "leftovers" are found in every aspect of our family lives.

For example, do you insist your kids get nine hours of sleep but you're lucky if you run on five?

Do you buy new clothes for your children but only shop thrift stores for yourself (if you shop for yourself at all)?

Do you schedule play dates and softball games and karate tournaments for the kids but put off planning meaningful visits with your own friends because, hey, who has time for that when you're all running your kids everywhere?

Do you keep the pediatrician on speed dial but refuse to take yourself to the doctor when you catch the same crud from your kids? Bonus points if you've actually finished off their pinkeye drops instead of getting a prescription for your own.

And do you give your time, energy, and attention to your children, your husband, your dog for crying out loud *all day long* but then feel guilty for wanting an hour to yourself?

You're not alone. Too many of us treat ourselves like second-class citizens within our own families. I'm great at this—or at least I used to be. And here is what I've learned the hard way.

Yes, it's good to give. It's good to serve. It's good to love selflessly and humbly.

But it's not good to treat yourself like poo.

(That's a quote. Write it down.)

The problem with many of us loving moms is that we'll give to our kids what we won't give to ourselves. They get the goods and we get the scraps. They flourish while we falter. Why? Because it's our job to care for our children, right?! God gave us this responsibility, and we are going to take it seriously. I mean, these youngsters aren't even ours! They're His! They are God's very own children!

Ah yes. They are.

But so are you.

And far be it from any of us moms to treat one of God's children like poo.

(Another quote. I am so eloquent.)

God values sacrifice, absolutely. But he values your relationship more.

I want you to show love, not offer sacrifices. I want you to know me more than I want burnt offerings.

Hosea 6:6 NLT

It's hard to be in a healthy relationship with God when you're burnt out. When you're feeding yourself junk and sleeping like a zombie and devaluing the person God created within your human shell. You are a mother, yes—a good one. Yet you are first and foremost God's treasured possession.

So tell me. How are you treating it lately?

You are worth more than your children's leftovers. Not in a sense of entitlement or indulgence, but because when we serve and give at the consistent expense of our own needs, we quickly erode our ability to serve and give *well*. Which makes us no good for anybody—our kids especially.

Good moms take care of their children.

Great moms take care of themselves, too.

Now let's talk about *how*.

Four Steps to Self-care

1. Prioritize your health. Once upon a time I neglected my body's warning signs that something wasn't quite right—stomach pains, woozy spells, tingling in my arms and legs—until they eventually landed me in the ER for a series of tests that all pointed to one enigmatic diagnosis: stress.

For real, hospital people? Just tell me you need to take out my gallbladder or something, please—anything but "stress," which really means there's nothing wrong with me except *everything* about the way I live my entire blessed life.

So I started taking my health more seriously. Today I eat better. I exercise. I see a nurse practitioner, a chiropractor, an enzyme therapist and, for a while, a Christian counselor—all in an effort to conquer this stress thing that so many of us have and ignore like it's no big deal. I spend time at these appointments. I spend money. I make sacrifices. Why? Because God created my body, His Spirit dwells within it, and I am determined to respect His masterpiece.

Your health needs might be different from mine, but we all have them. Self-care begins with tending to our physical and mental well-being. If you've been neglecting your body and mind, please, choose to make a change. Pray about it. Find someone you trust to hold you accountable. God can use our physical and emotional challenges to draw us closer to Him. Perhaps it's one of the reasons He allows disease. So take Him up on His offer. Walk toward healing—with the Lord in the lead.

> Let all that I am praise the Lord; may I never forget the good things he does for me. He forgives all my sins and heals all my diseases. He redeems me from death and crowns me with love and tender mercies. He fills my life with good things. My youth is renewed like the eagle's!
>
> Psalm 103:2–5 NLT

2. Find what fuels you. We all need to replenish our spirits, but how we do it depends on who we are. I'm an introvert, so for me an hour spent reading quietly by myself is like a slice of heaven in the middle of a devilish day. For you, maybe that hour is better spent in a room full of chatty women sharing a bottle of wine and snorting laughter.

What do you enjoy? What lifts your spirit and calms your soul? I asked my Facebook friends to share their favorite "me time" activity, and the list was as diverse as the women themselves. They cited everything from scrapbooking, singing, crocheting, and gardening to waterskiing, hiking, kickboxing, and dancing. Lots of women mentioned simple pleasures like napping, hot showers, watching Netflix, and roaming the Target aisles with a to-go cup of coffee in hand. (Yes! I'm not the only one!) My friend Hilary—a busy mom and sales guru with an inhuman schedule—discovered pickleball games at our church gym.

—Creative Ways to Find Time— for Yourself

- Keep a book, a Bible, or your knitting (it's totally back in vogue)—whatever you choose—in your purse or car and sneak a few minutes to enjoy it while you wait in the carpool line, at dance class, piano lessons, halftime, etc. Chauffeuring our kids all over God's green earth can have its advantages.
- Strike a baby-sitting deal with a friend. Choose someone whose kids get along well with yours, then schedule play dates in which only one mom needs to be present. That means once a week you take her kids for a couple hours, then the following week she takes your kids for a couple hours, and so on. Consider setting a ground rule that *VeggieTales* movies are a perfectly acceptable form of fellowship for the children during these get-togethers.
- Find a gym that offers childcare as part of your membership. Drop the kids off, exercise for thirty minutes, then spend another hour or two taking a leisurely shower or reading a book at the smoothie bar.
- While the kids are at school, take a couple hours off to go to a movie or a coffee shop by yourself.
- If you have small children in the house, set aside a special toy bin filled with safe, non-messy activities that the kids enjoy but are only allowed to play with during "room time." Set the timer for one hour of quiet play in their bedrooms while you take a breather in yours.

"What I love about playing pickleball is I can completely let go of all outside responsibilities and just focus on the game and have fun with my friends," Hilary said. "Because it's a fast-paced and strategic sport, my thoughts can't wander back to my to-do list like

- If you work outside the home, spend your lunch breaks at a park where you can sit and clear your head, listen to worship music, or call a good friend to catch up.
- Does your church offer a Bible study with childcare? Go.
- If you're married and your husband is willing, sync electronic calendars and block time for yourself. This works best as a reciprocal deal. Create an event code word that you agree means "I need this time or I will go crazy," then cover for one another's escape.
- Form a monthly book club or scrapbooking group and pool together your resources to hire a babysitter or two for everyone's kiddos. You can enjoy a couple hours of adult fellowship while the kids have their own play time in another part of the house.
- During the summer, institute thirty to sixty minutes of mandatory reading time in the early afternoon. Then go to your own room and close the door.
- If you're a morning person, set your alarm to rise an hour or two before your children wake up. If your kids are prone to thwarting this plan, set a timer on their night-light and teach them they cannot come out of their rooms until that light goes off in the morning.
- If your littles struggle to fall asleep without you, use their bedtime to your advantage. Sit in their room with a flashlight and read your Bible while they fall asleep. I did this for a season in time, and I assure you my children did not turn out socially dependent because of it. Now that they're older, I can't believe I'm saying this, but—I miss those sweet hours.

they often do throughout the day. It's the only time I truly check out 100 percent, and when I check back in, my heart is filled and my mind feels rebooted, focused, and ready to go!"

I know. You all want to Google pickleball now, don't you? Just listening to Hilary talk about the game, I'm tempted to join the league myself. But that's the point.

Our "me time" activities should fill our soul tanks with an ample supply of energy and joy that we can then pour into all the other areas of our lives—family, work, ministry, and so on. Find what fuels you. And then . . .

   3. Schedule time to do it. There are plenty of obstacles to "me time." Babies wake in the night, stealing our sleep. Husbands travel, leaving us homebound on solo mom duty. Daily responsibilities often leave very little margin in which we can halt the madness and drink a Diet Coke on the veranda. An important aspect of pursuing self-care is to first redefine what it is.

Self-care is not a luxury. It's a necessity. Therefore, we ought to schedule it into our calendars just as we do the grocery shopping or the oil change. If you have a hard time making room for self-care, then treat it as you would any other priority. Plan ahead.

Not sure how to start? Examine your calendar and determine where you can squeeze in fifteen minutes for yourself this week. Spend that time reading or taking a bath or walking around the block, whatever helps you unwind. Eventually, if you can, increase to thirty minutes or an hour daily. Coordinate calendars with your husband or a mom friend and support one another's need for downtime. Then try not to allow ordinary tasks or pressures to trump your planned rest. The laundry never goes away, so it can wait until you're back from your stroll through Target.

   4. Give yourself grace. I hate exercising. I really do. I know women who live for the rush of jogging, spinning, or benching half their body weight, and I'm telling you, that kind of passion is foreign to me. I'd rather sit at home eating popcorn.

But—I drag my butt to the gym anyway, because I know my forty-something carcass needs exercise in order to stay healthy. Unfortunately, because my family/work/ministry schedule keeps me booked solid between the hours of 7 a.m. and 8 p.m. most weekdays, the only time I can attend an exercise class is 6 a.m. Not ideal, but again, I do it for the sake of self-care. Usually.

Except for those mornings when I'm particularly wiped or under the weather or just generally needing a little extra sleep. Then I skip the gym—(gasp!)—oh yes, I do. Why? Because rest and exercise are both on my list of self-care musts. Therefore, I give myself permission not to neglect one over the other.

Listen to your body. Know what it needs on any given day. Stay disciplined, yes, but not at the expense of the whole purpose—which is preventing burnout and refueling your soul. Sometimes the very best way to take care of *you* is to give yourself a day off. And do it without remorse.

Remember Your Greatest Need

Finally, sisters, do not forget that your most essential source of strength and renewal comes from the One who knows your body and soul even better than you do—because He created it.

> Do you not know? Have you not heard? The Lord is the everlasting God, the Creator of the ends of the earth. He will not grow tired or weary, and his understanding no one can fathom. He gives strength to the weary and increases the power of the weak. Even youths grow tired and weary, and young men stumble and fall; but those who hope in the Lord will renew their strength. They will soar on wings like eagles; they will run and not grow weary, they will walk and not be faint.
>
> Isaiah 40:28–31

Those who hope in the Lord will renew their strength. The Hebrew root word for *hope* here is *qâvâh*, which means "to wait for, or to look for with eager expectation."[1] It's not a passive term but rather an action—the ongoing choice to seek and trust God in our everyday, imperfect lives. We do this every time we crack open a Bible or attend a Bible study or pray. When we make time for the Lord, we invite Him to restore us. When we don't, we wither. Therefore, the very best way to take care of yourself is to stay close to Jesus. He alone can repair and rejuvenate your deeply tired soul.

> I am the vine; you are the branches. If you remain in me and I in you, you will bear much fruit; apart from me you can do nothing.
>
> John 15:5

 *Let's Dig In!*

1. Revisit Psalm 127:1–2 (TLB): "Unless the Lord builds a house, the builders' work is useless. Unless the Lord protects a city, sentries do no good. It is senseless for you to work so hard from early morning until late at night, fearing you will starve to death; for God wants his loved ones to get their proper rest." In what ways do we try to "play God" in our busy lives? How does this affect our moods, our health, and our relationships?

2. Deuteronomy 4:9 (ESV) says, "Only take care, and keep your soul diligently, lest you forget the things that your eyes have seen, and lest they depart from your heart all the days of your life. Make them known to your children and your children's children." What does it mean to "keep your soul diligently"?

3. How does caring for ourselves help us focus on God and His provision, i.e., "the things that your eyes have seen"? Whom are we commanded to teach about these things? How can the state of our physical and mental health affect our ability to do it well?

4. Read Proverbs 4:20–22 and Proverbs 3:7–8. In what ways does God's wisdom—knowing Him and His Bible truths—bring health to your body? Please understand that studying the Bible is not some magic elixir against disease. People of

strong faith still face illness and hardship. Jesus warned us, "In this world you will have trouble. But take heart! I have overcome the world" (John 16:33). What does this mean to you? How can a close relationship with Jesus help us through times of sickness, crisis, or fatigue?

5. Read Philippians 4:6–7. Do you struggle with worry, anxiety, or stress? How does this affect your overall state of well-being? According to this Scripture, God clearly cares about our hearts and minds—our emotional and mental health. What does He want us to do when we're struggling? What does He promise in return?

6. Jesus modeled the importance of rest and solitude, especially in order to spend quiet time with God. Read Mark 1:35; Luke 5:15–16; Luke 6:12; Mark 6:31–32; and Matthew 14:23. If even Jesus needed a reprieve from time to time, imagine how much more we imperfect mortals also need a break to rest, refuel, and pray. How does this truth affect your attitude toward self-care? Does your own life reflect Jesus' priorities? Why or why not?

7. Revisit Isaiah 40:28–41. Verses 30–31 say, "Even youths grow tired and weary, and young men stumble and fall; but those who hope in the Lord will renew their strength." When we see the word *but* or *yet* in Scripture, we should pause and ponder the preceding text. God is presenting a statement of contrast. Here He's comparing youths—young men of vigor and physical strength—with the "hopers," or those who trust in the Lord to be their supernatural strength. In whose strength do you go about your busy day—yours or God's? What does it mean to you to live in God's strength?

8. How can we maintain a focus on Jesus even in the midst of busy days or time-consuming responsibilities? Consider that when God is truly our priority, He is woven into every aspect of our daily lives. What do the following verses tell us about a God-centric life?

- What we think: Isaiah 26:3; 2 Corinthians 10:5; Psalm 19:14
- What we value: Colossians 3:1; Matthew 6:21; Matthew 6:33
- How we speak: James 3:9–10; Matthew 15:8; Colossians 4:6
- What we know: Psalm 119:11; 2 Timothy 3:16–17; James 1:25

Meet Them Where They Are

"Do you realize how many events, choices, that had to occur since the birth of the universe leading up to the making of you? Just exactly the way you are." —*A Wrinkle in Time*

6

Your Child Is Not You

My friend Emily is raising a literal thinker. Her son is wired to hear and process words as facts, void of nuance or suggestion. For example, one day she told him, "Myles, please put my shoes on the shelf in my room."

Emily recounted to me, "I meant the shoe rack, which is, of course, filled with shoes." Instead, Myles carefully placed two pairs of his mom's shoes on a small decorative bookshelf five feet away from the shoe rack. "When I explained to him I meant the shoe rack, he told me, 'You said *shelf*, Mom, not rack. So I put them on the shelf.'"

Do you ever have trouble communicating with your children? I sure do. Many parents struggle in one way or another to get through to their beloved apples, whether they fall close to the tree or look altogether more like a banana. This can cause a lot of frustration for parents and kids alike.

I'm here to share a solution I've learned through Bible studies, trial and error, and godly wisdom from mentor moms. It's vital to our goal of becoming kinder, gentler parents. On the surface, the secret to communicating effectively with our kids might actually be quite simple.

Think like a kid.

But not just any kid.

Think like *your* kid.

Ah, that's the tricky part, isn't it? Because thinking like our kids requires knowing them, observing them, studying them, and tending to them on a whole new level—*their* level. Their personal, God-designed, one-of-a-kind level.

Do you truly understand your child? Are you tuned in to her emotions, disposition, triggers, and needs?

Do you see your son or daughter as an individual with unique qualities that can be nurtured for great purposes?

Do you trust the God of the universe to shape your children into the people He intends them to be—in spite of your failures and victories?

If you cannot yet answer a wholehearted "yes" to these questions, then stick with me, sister. In the next several chapters, we're going to explore how to enter our children's world so we can meet them where they are. This will enable us to guide and encourage them in a way that makes sense to their hearts and minds, which can then mitigate a host of frustrations for everyone. The first step is to recognize a huge, yet not-so-obvious truth: Your child is not you.

Who Are These People?

When you were pregnant or praying for the child God would bring to your family through adoption, who did you picture? What did you imagine your child's temperament would be? How did you envision his interests, talents, tendencies, sense of humor?

Now compare that kid with the one living in your house. Are they the same—or vastly different?

Our children are unique individuals, wonderfully designed by a perfect Creator who has never made a mistake. That means your son or daughter is exactly who he or she is supposed to be.

Trouble comes when, whether overtly or subconsciously, we place expectations on our children according to our own personalities and preferences. Then we risk harboring certain presumptions about how they are "supposed" to think or act, regardless of how that gels with what God actually created.

Understand, I'm not talking about disobedience here. We must train our children to obey and follow Jesus, of course. But there's a lot of room for varying personalities within the parameters of godly living.

For example, maybe you expected your child to love basketball but he prefers painting. Maybe you wish your daughter was quiet and demure but God programmed her to seek adventures. Maybe you hoped your kids would flip for roller coasters and bumper cars and rock climbing but they really just want to stay home and read. Is that so terrible?

Critical to communicating effectively with our children is a willingness to understand and accept who they really are—which is to say, who God designed them to be. As moms, our challenge is to embrace the individuals God created and discover how to nurture them accordingly. It begins with separating our own identity from theirs.

Mini-Me: If Your Child's Personality Is Similar to Yours

One of my girls is a lot like me. She's a planner, a list-maker, a creative yet methodical thinker. She loves to sing and write songs and take photos for her blog. (Yes, she has a blog—a girl after her momma's own heart.)

When her feelings are hurt and she melts into a puddle of tears on her bed, I know why without having to ask. I can knock gently on the door, sit on the edge of her mattress, and carefully coax out her heartache because speaking to her is like speaking to myself at that age. We get each other.

Which is also why she drives me absolutely batty. Because sometimes she reflects my less-favorable qualities as well, like my perfectionism, my anxiety, my habit of running late, my fear of calling people on the telephone (it's a thing, okay?). I look at her and I see the flawed parts of myself, and I want to save her from the consequences. *Don't do it, baby! Don't be like your mother! Run, now, while there's still hope for you!*

But the fact is, my daughter is not me. I cannot learn her lessons for her. The best I can do is offer guidance and wisdom from my own experience, then allow her to rise or fall of her own volition. Her free will is a gift from God, and He will chisel her through her choices just as He chisels me through mine. My job is to trust Him.

So for those of us who struggle at times to parent the child who is most like us, consider this: Your child is expertly fashioned by God. And so are you. Next time you're fed up with your mini-me, ask yourself—am I upset with her, or am I upset with me? Then extend a big Jesus-sized dose of grace to both of you.

> For you created my inmost being; you knit me together in my mother's womb. I praise you because I am fearfully and wonderfully made; your works are wonderful, I know that full well.
>
> Psalm 139:13–14

Polar Opposites: If Your Child's Personality Is Different from Yours

Remember middle school? My sixth-grade class was a pack of crocodiles poised to snap and devour one another.

If a girl's hair was too stringy or her pants weren't in style, she got kicked out of the "group" (a.k.a. swamp).

If her science test score was too high, blowing the curve for all the other kids who didn't bother to study, she was labeled a "brainiac" and left to sit alone at lunch.

If Jenny liked Jason but Jason skated with Carla at the roller rink, well, Carla, too, was *out*. Shunned. Targeted. Made fun of—

until Jenny also breached some ever-shifting code of conduct, in which case Carla was back in but only until Jenny could redeem her popularity by spreading rumors that Carla liked Brian—and everybody knows what a dweeb Brian is, so, case closed.

Man, I hated those years.

Naturally, now that my daughters have reached tweendom, I'm determined to keep close tabs on their hearts, their relationships, and their social climate *so that* maybe, just maybe Mom can help, Mom can advise, Mom can preempt the formative pain of growing up female in America where girls are mean and recess is hostile territory.

Except. My older daughter doesn't care.

This child has such iron-clad confidence, not only does she rarely get rattled by others kids' snarkiness, I suspect she doesn't even recognize it in the first place.

She thinks everybody is friends with everybody, and everybody is a friend to her.

How can a child be so oblivious to the drama?

Thank God she is oblivious to the drama.

In this sense, I want to be like my daughter.

But I'm not.

I am the girl who *still* cares too much about what other people think, what other people say, how other people are sizing me up and cutting me down. So in a well-meaning effort to guide my daughter through social relationships, my tendency is to impose my own worldview—and my own issues—on my child's situation.

Which doesn't actually help her at all.

"Sweetie, how was hot lunch today? Did you like the ravioli?" I'll pose an innocent question like this after school.

"Yeah, it was really good." And because she is an eleven-year-old girl, she elaborates. "I sat with Ava and Kendra, and they had cold lunch, and when they saw my tray they kept saying they wish they'd signed up for hot lunch today, too. They were like, hey, give me a bite, please? Just one bite? It was sooooo funny."

My mom radar lights up.

"You sat by Ava and Kendra? Where was Maggie?"

"Oh, she was sitting with Emma and some other girls at a different table."

"But I thought you always sit with Maggie. Are you still hanging out with Maggie?"

"Yeah, Mom! We're all good friends."

"Well, how long has it been since you sat with Maggie at lunch?"

"I don't know. I just sit wherever."

"Is Emma nice to you?"

"Yes! We're all friends!"

"Do you and Maggie still play together at recess?"

"Sometimes."

"Who did you play with today?"

"Ava and Kendra."

Not Maggie? Your sweet friend Maggie?? Why doesn't she want to hang out with you? Is it Emma? That little rat. Is she stealing my daughter's friends?? I need to have a talk with her mother!

"Mom?"

"Yes, sweetheart?"

"Why are you asking me all these questions? Can I have a snack now?"

Ugh. Clearly the only person in this scenario who needs guidance is me. When I assume my daughter thinks and feels as I would, not only am I not helping, but I might actually be planting hurtful ideas in her head, such as, *Maggie doesn't like you anymore, darling. But don't worry. Momma's here. I'll always love you. Let's go eat hot fudge sundaes.*

My friend Kelley can relate.

"I was very social when I was young," she told me, "so to me, 'normal' for a teen meant going out every weekend to be with friends." However, Kelley's daughter often stayed home instead. Kelley started worrying she was having friendship problems or possibly suffering from depression.

"It was her freshman year, and she was home again on a Friday night, so I probed about it," Kelley said. "I meant to be supportive, but what she heard me ask was, 'What's wrong with you that you don't have plans on a Friday night?' And she responded quietly, 'Is it okay if I don't want to go out? Is it okay if I like to be home?' I was dumbfounded! I mean, why wouldn't a kid want to have plans on the weekend? Why would she want to stay home, here, with her parents and three younger siblings? I just could not identify with that."

Through many open-hearted conversations, Kelley eventually learned her daughter wasn't struggling socially; she just preferred to spend weekends taking a much-needed break from the pressures of high school. And she actually enjoyed her siblings more than her friends!

"Once I realized this was not a sign of teen depression but just a big difference in our personalities, I was able to relax and embrace it," Kelley said.

Now that her daughter is grown and married, Kelley is especially grateful for the time they spent together during those high school years. Their relationship grew stronger because Kelley was willing to step beyond her own point of view and truly get to know her child.

Follow Their Natural Bent

Proverbs 22:6 says, "Start children off on the way they should go, and even when they are old they will not turn from it." The question is, which way is "the way"?

Generally speaking, Proverbs is a book about wisdom—where to find it and why it's worth getting. So "the way" in which we should train our children is toward God and His truth, the source of all wisdom. We do that largely by living out our own faith at home, demonstrating kindness and acceptance and forgiveness and grace—you know, all the stuff this book is aiming for. You're already on that path. Keep going. I'm right here with you.

More specifically, though, the Hebrew rendering of "the way" is the word *dereck*, which in English translates as *bents*. Therefore, training children in "the way they should go" means raising them according to their natural inclinations. In one of my favorite books, *Grace Based Parenting*, author Dr. Tim Kimmel explains:

> If you were making a bow out of a tree limb, you'd first study the limb to figure out what its natural "bent" is. Then you'd string it. If you didn't do this, when you pulled the bow back, it would snap because it was strung against its natural bent rather than with it. In the same way, we are to groom our children according to their natural bents. This means coming alongside them with a plan to help leverage their *natural* and *unique* gifts and skills into highly developed assets that they can lean on in the future.[1]

This is why we must get to know and appreciate who our children are as individuals, separate from our own biases or expectations. Only then can we truly encourage them to reach their full, God-given potential. And—here's a bonus. We'll grow nearer to our own potential in the process.

My friend Tynea can testify.

My husband and I refer to our second child as his child. They are exactly the same, and I am the complete opposite of them. She is a social butterfly, and she moves nonstop. I am an introvert who can sit still for hours. She pushes every boundary there is, and I'm a rule follower. Parenting her has been a huge stretch—completely different from my firstborn, whom I understand because she is a lot like me. I know what makes her tick. I know how to handle her reactions to different situations because I experience those same reactions. With my younger daughter, I have felt more than once that I was not cut out to be her mother. How am I supposed to parent someone I don't understand?

It has not been an easy journey, but it has been a season of incredible growth. By taking the time to study and embrace my second daughter's character, I get to see who God created her to be. She's not me. She's not going to do things the way I would, and that's not a bad thing. She has an incredible heart and such passion. Seeing the differences between us makes me realize how amazing God is at crafting each person with a unique purpose. The people she's going to reach in this life are going to be completely different than the people I would reach, and I love that. I can honestly say, even through all the struggles, it is an honor to be her mom.

Is It All Up to Me?

One more word of encouragement—or caution, depending on how you see it. Many of us will read the second half of Proverbs 22:6—"even when they are old they will not turn from it"—and interpret those words as a pinky-swear promise from God.

If I raise my children right, then they will grow up to be holy.

If I discipline with grace and install parental controls on the computer and give them a purity ring when they turn thirteen, then they will never try drugs or cheat on an exam or have sex before marriage.

And if I pray for them and teach them Scripture and send them to Sunday school or youth group or Christian college all their growing-up years, then they will not stray from the faith.

Yes! If I—the loving, intentional parent—do A plus B plus C, then D will surely follow because GOD SAYS SO!

Except—not quite. Read the rest of Proverbs and you'll quickly discover our choices have just as much bearing on our future as our upbringing does. It's evident in verses like these:

If you are wise, your wisdom will reward you; if you are a mocker, you alone will suffer.

Proverbs 9:12

The wise in heart accept commands, but a chattering fool comes to ruin.

Proverbs 10:8

Those who trust in themselves are fools, but those who walk in wisdom are kept safe.

Proverbs 28:26

As parents, we must step back at some critical point and let our children make their own decisions, whether foolish or wise. It's a necessary part of them maturing and making their faith their own. Yes, they might get hurt. They might stumble. We might all have regrets one day, regardless of how hard we worked at raising our children "right." But God is sovereign. He can redeem bad choices and broken people. It's His specialty.

So whoever our children are today and whoever they will become tomorrow, remember God has them covered at a level we mortal moms can't possibly reach this side of heaven. He is their all-knowing, forever faithful, almighty Father—the perfect parent. And I'm so grateful for that.

I rest in that.

Will you?

 *Let's Dig In!*

1. Do you have a child whose personality is very different from yours? Or one that is quite similar? What challenges do you face in parenting that child? How did the principles we learned in this chapter provide some insight into overcoming those challenges?

2. Read Deuteronomy 32:3–4; Psalm 18:30; Psalm 19:7; and Hebrews 4:15. What do these verses tell you about God?
   - He is perfect.
   - He is just.
   - He is without sin.

— Fun Family Conversation Starters —

Want to get to know your kids better? Start with these fun questions to spark conversation around the dinner table. The whole family will have a blast using their imagination and critical thinking skills while also learning something new about one another. For added giggles, try to guess how each family member will answer! And—don't forget to follow up every question with "why?"

- If you could eat only one food for the rest of your life, what would it be?
- What forest animal would you choose for a pet?
- If you could talk with any character in the Bible, who would you choose? (If anyone says Jesus, let them also pick a second person. Jesus is usually the obvious choice!)
- Would you rather be able to fly or turn invisible?
- Would you rather ride to school on an elephant or in a giant shopping cart?
- What one question would you like to ask God?
- If you could create your own cereal, what would it be called? What would it taste like?
- Would you rather live in the jungle, the desert, the ocean, or the North Pole?
- If you could visit any time in history, which would you choose?
- If you had to wear clothing of only one color for a year, which color would you pick?
- Would you rather be strong, smart, rich, or happy?

All of the above! A common statement among Christians is, "God makes no mistakes." And the Scriptures confirm this is true. Consider your child's personality and abilities. Even if your child tends to use these traits or abilities to sin at times (as we all do), the core of who he/she is was designed on purpose, for a purpose, by a loving and flawless God. How does this truth alter the way you view your children?

3. Now refer to Ephesians 2:10. I like the New Living Translation of this verse: "For we are God's masterpiece. He has created us anew in Christ Jesus, so we can do the good things he planned for us long ago." Do you realize your child is a masterpiece? Psalm 139:13–14 further asserts that our kids are "wonderfully made." In what ways do you question why your children are the way they are? In what ways have you doubted God's goodness in granting you a strong-willed child, or a painfully shy child, or a special needs child, etc.? Spend some time in prayer, asking God to help you see your children the way He sees them.

4. See Jeremiah 1:5 and Galatians 1:15. Both the prophet Jeremiah and the apostle Paul recognized that God called them, even before they were born, to do His work on earth. God himself speaks to Jeremiah confirming this. Ephesians 2:10 applies this same principle to all believers, saying there are certain "good things"—tasks, service, accomplishments, worship, etc.—that God planned for us long ago. This is true for me and you, and it's true for our children. As parents, we are invited to nurture, train, and equip our kids to fulfill God's plans for their lives. One of the most important prayers we can pray over our children is that God would help us see who He wants them to be, and then give us the courage and wisdom to guide them toward His will. Is this easy or difficult for you? Why?

5. Do you wonder if it's possible our children could miss God's plan for their lives? Or that it's possible for us to thwart it somehow with our "bad" parenting? Be encouraged. Although we do have free will, and our decisions certainly carry consequences, God's Word makes it clear that He is in control and will work all things out for our good—even our bad decisions. See Isaiah 14:27; Proverbs 16:9; Proverbs

21:30; and Romans 8:28. How do these verses speak to your heart today?

6. As parents we have a wonderful opportunity to empower our kids to love and trust God, so they will one day seek His will even more than they seek our advice. The best way to teach this is by modeling that love and trust in our own lives. Do you find it difficult to rely on God's faithfulness to lead and protect your children, particularly when His plan is different from your plan? Why or why not? Like we've already discussed, God makes no mistakes. See Proverbs 3:5–6, and ask God to help you trust Him more than your own understanding.

7. Read James 1:19. The Bible says we should be quick to listen, not speak. Do you regularly stop to listen to your children before you speak? How could doing so help you understand them better?

8. Name one concern that each of your children is facing right now. How have you been encouraging (or exasperating) your child in this area? Often we can become impatient or dismissive when a child's concern seems minor or irrational to our adult reasoning. Yet to them, it's reality. In order to encourage them, we need to humble ourselves and enter their world. Consider writing a letter to each of your children—and your husband if needed—addressing their particular fear or concern using only healing, encouraging words. If your kids aren't reading yet, set them on your lap the next time the concern comes up, and tell them they can count on you to help. For example, "I know you're afraid of the dark. But did you know God made the light and the dark, and He called it all good? God knows you are safe in your bed, and so does Mom. I understand sometimes you don't feel that way, though. Let's pray for God to help you be brave!"

7

Have Some Respect

In first-century Bible times, parents loved their children just as we do today. Yet the culture in general didn't value them very much. Kids were considered a burden to society until they were old enough to earn their keep. Even Jesus' own disciples presumed not to "bother" the Son of God with a child's needs.

> People were bringing little children to Jesus for him to place his hands on them, but the disciples rebuked them. When Jesus saw this, he was indignant. He said to them, "Let the little children come to me, and do not hinder them, for the kingdom of God belongs to such as these. Truly I tell you, anyone who will not receive the kingdom of God like a little child will never enter it."
>
> Mark 10:13–15

Don't you just adore Jesus? He wasn't simply irritated with His disciples—He was indignant. Blowing off little ones proved profoundly offensive to Him. What does this tell us about the value God places on children? They're not a burden in His eyes. On the contrary, He names them the very heirs to His kingdom. What an amazing status regardless of age.

So let me ask. How do you view your own children? Oh, of course you love them. I love mine, too. But I've got to admit—sometimes I treat them like second-class citizens.

Do this, don't do that, fetch me this, don't bother me with that. It's easy to bark orders as though my kids exist to serve me and to jump at all my interjectory commands. In this way, I'm afraid I regard them as underlings rather than vital members of the family. And that's just not right.

Our children are people, too. They deserve the same respect we'd give any child of God—whether eight years old or eighty.

Now, please understand what I'm *not* saying. Respecting our kids doesn't mean we should let them run the show. Again, God calls us to "bring them up in the training and instruction of the Lord" (Ephesians 6:4), and that involves plenty of teaching, correcting, redirecting, and discipline. I'm also not suggesting we put children on a pedestal or allow our homes to revolve around them. The Bible makes it clear there is a pecking order in our relationships: God, marriage, then children. (See this chapter's Let's Dig In! questions for more details on that important truth.)

The question is—*how* are we training our children? *How* are we raising them up for the kingdom? Are we giving our kids the same dignity that Jesus gives them? Or have we slipped into the habit of pushing them around?

The Bible warns us not to abuse our authority as parents. The Amplified Bible puts it this way:

> Fathers, do not provoke or irritate or exasperate your children [with demands that are trivial or unreasonable or humiliating or abusive; nor by favoritism or indifference; treat them tenderly with loving-kindness], so they will not lose heart and become discouraged or unmotivated [with their spirits broken].
>
> Colossians 3:21 AMP

Ouch. I'm afraid I've done my share of spirit breaking over the years, have you? How can a mom turn it around? How can we prevent or repair discouragement and begin treating our children consistently with the kindness and respect they deserve?

From my own experience, here are six powerful solutions I've found.

1. Learn Your Child's Love Language

In order to speak love and encouragement to a child's heart, we first need to know what types of words or actions the child interprets as most loving. It's called his love language. Some of you may be familiar with this concept—and I've surely written about it before—but we could all use a good refresher. According to *The 5 Love Languages of Children* by Gary Chapman, people of all ages tend to receive love best in one of five ways:

- Receiving gifts
- Quality time
- Word of affirmation
- Acts of service
- Physical touch[1]

My younger daughter's primary love language is receiving gifts. A piece of chocolate or a new pack of markers can brighten her mood in seconds. My older daughter, however, prefers quality time. She'd rather take a trip to Starbucks for a mom/daughter date where we can chat one-on-one without interruptions.

Imagine then if I gave the pack of markers to my firstborn and the Starbucks date to my younger babe. I might intend to say, "Look how much Mom loves you!" but their hearts would hear it louder if I had switched the gifts.

Figure out what your child's love language is (take the quiz on 5lovelanguages.com), then speak it as best you can. This alone can break barriers and build a stronger, kinder rapport with your children.

2. Allow Kids to Be Kids

Proverbs 22:15 says, "Folly is bound up in the heart of a child," and as moms we witness this truth every day. Kids do dumb stuff. They draw pictures on the wall with Sharpies. They give the dog a haircut. They're absolutely sure it would be a good idea to ride down the basement stairs on snowboards—until the ER nurse explains why it's not.

As mature adults, it's easy for us to scold our children for being foolish, as if they should know better. But they don't. Sometimes they truly don't know the difference between a good and bad idea simply because they're kids, and foolishness is part of their natural state. Can you relate to these stories?

"When our triplets were three, they thought it would be funny to drop our newly acquired kittens down our second-story clothes chute. Fortunately, I was never caught up on laundry, so the kittens had a very soft pile to land on when they fell to the basement floor."—Amanda

"My kids put a quarter in the DVD slot of my van. That was a $235 'experiment.'"—Mary Beth

"I told my son to clean his room, which he wasn't thrilled about. So he thought he'd found a shortcut by tossing everything out the window. Until it started raining."—Renee

"My dear son and his best pal flushed Lego guys and then socks down the toilet, then stuck their heads in and shampooed—with big sister's expensive shampoo, no less."
—Rachel

"My kids used the back of the tub as a water slide. They also aimed the bathtub whirlpool jets so the water would shoot into the bathroom. Both these adventures resulted in water dripping down the light fixtures on the first floor."
—Debbie

"My son held up a pea at the dinner table and announced, 'Now you see it, now you don't,' and shoved the pea up his nose to complete his magic trick before we could stop him."
—Brooke

"My two-year-old daughter hid my car keys—twice—and forgot where she put them."—Tynea

"My son and his friend painted our front porch—and each other—with model airplane paint. I won't tell you what I needed to use to get it off their bodies because soap didn't work!"—Patricia

Hilarious, right? Yet each of these parents would tell you their child's antics were not so funny at the time. It's easy to let frustration take over and scold our kids for behaviors that we, as adults, could have predicted would not turn out well. It's much harder to stay calm and approach ignorance as a teaching opportunity. But it is possible. Here are four steps to redeeming those "what were you thinking?!" moments.

- Immediately call to mind the fact that "folly is bound up in the heart of a child." Remind yourself—foolishness is normal for kids. It's expected! They are just doing what kids do. Breathe in, breathe out, and prepare to address the issue armed with self-control rather than unchecked anger.
- Discern if your child knew right from wrong in this situation. If you're sure he did, then hang on for chapters 11 and

12, where we'll discuss how to handle willful disobedience. For now we're focusing on "dumb" but not necessarily rebellious behavior.

As the adult, for example, we don't need anybody to tell us tossing kitties down the laundry chute is a bad idea. However, kids don't yet know this inherently. And chances are we parents have never actually spelled out a rule to match the offense—because who could predict the need to warn against extreme cat sports? If a child is not yet mentally or socially mature enough to discern a particular right from wrong on his own, then we cannot hold the child to our adult standards. Unfortunately, our kids—and their bewildered parents—must learn many boundaries by trial and error. It's our job to help them do that.

• Teach before you punish. Unless your child's dumb choice was a serious safety issue, try to refrain from swift discipline. First explain why this action was unwise. Ask questions. Get inside your child's head and try to determine what was going on in that amazing brain of his. Children are fascinating. They're creative. And as parents we have the privilege of unearthing that creativity, affirming it, nurturing it, and showing our kids how to channel it for good purposes. Who knows how handling their wacky ideas with gentle guidance might inspire them to one day use their (more mature) wacky ideas for God's glory?

• Finally, for those days when you really want to scream, remember this humbling truth: We were kids once, too. And we were no smarter than our children.

"When I was two and my brother was three, he cut off half of one pigtail. We both thought we were just playing barber and the pigtail could be put back."—Heidi

"When I was a kid my mom washed all the windows outside of the home. I saw her doing it and found a rag in

my play house and followed behind her reaching as high as I could go with the dirty rag. Needless to say, she had to rewash the windows once I caught up to her."—Saija

"When I was younger, I didn't believe the cartoons that showed people slipping on banana peels, so I tried it for myself, obviously to prove that it was not slippery. Guess what happened? I ran straight for the peel, stepped on it, and fell flat on my back. Turns out they are slippery!"—Karley

"When my brother was around five years old, he thought that by holding on to plastic grocery bags in each hand he could jump from the top of the swing set and soar to the ground casually as if using a parachute. He bruised his heel bones so bad that he still walks on his toes. He's almost thirty."
—Amy

3. Don't Make Your Child Your Slave

For years I dreamed of hiring a cleaning lady. Until my daughter grew old enough to become one.

"Mom, do you have any chores to do today? Anything I can help with?" My then six-year-old clasped her hands beneath her chin and grinned.

"Well, since you asked, I do need to clean the bathroom."

"(Gasp!) I love cleaning the bathroom! Can I scrub the toilet? Please, please?"

"Ah . . . sure." (Twist your momma's arm.) "Would you like to clean the tub, too?"

She ran straight for the sink cabinet and grabbed a scrub brush. "Just show me what to do, Mom!"

Well, hallelujah. Within an hour, my daughter had wiped, dusted, and swept half the house. Next I considered teaching her to fold laundry and bake a casserole, then maybe I could kick my feet up on the sofa, crack open a can of Pringles, and watch while she took over my job.

When we entered the school stage, I enjoyed seeing my firstborn gain independent skills. She could pour her own cereal, tie her own shoes, help shred lettuce, and answer the phone. But sometimes I confess I took a little too much advantage of her maturity.

> *"Sweetie, your sister is hungry. Can you get her some toast, please?"*
>
> *"Would you hand me my scissors, darling? Mom doesn't feel like getting up from this chair."*
>
> *"I need you to put away your backpack, your jacket, your shoes, your glasses, your hairbrush, your sister's shoes, your sister's hat, your sister's dolls, yesterday's dishes, this entire basket of clean towels, and a hoarder's stack of* Highlights *magazines that I never got around to organizing. And while you're at it, would you please teach your sister how to write her alphabet?"*

"But Moooom! I was in the middle of coloring this picture!"

Oops. I forgot. My daughter is not my slave. She's a kid. And she doesn't deserve to be treated like the help—especially when I'm just too lazy or distracted to do my own mom job.

Do you do it, too? Maybe it's time to cut our kids some slack and let them, once again, be kids. Chores are healthy, yes. God wants us to work heartily for Him (Colossians 3:23) and to serve one another (Galatians 5:13). Yet above all, the Bible tells us God is love. He is patient, compassionate, creative, and wise. So while it's important to encourage our kids to be selfless and hard-working, it's just as important to nurture creativity, autonomy, and self-expression. To give our kids space to discover not only what we're expecting them to do, but also who God created them to *be*. So let's not overburden them with responsibilities beyond what's fair.

4. Give a Five-Minute Warning

My husband used to be a human time bomb. He was a man on a schedule, and he did NOT like to run late. The trouble was, nobody else in the family could hear him ticking down. The only signal we'd get that it was time to move was the explosion itself.

"Car is running! Let's go!" He'd call from the garage entry door, while the rest of us were in various stages of preparing to leave the house—me in socks but no shoes, one child still chewing her pancakes while the other was curled in a ball on the sofa wearing nothing but underwear.

"A little warning, please?" I raised my eyebrows at the bomb.

"What, I thought we said we could be there by nine. It's time to go."

"Yes, but we never discussed how long it would take to get there. The girls are still eating breakfast."

"Gotcha." He tossed a couple granola bars in his pocket. "They can eat on the way. Let's go!"

This drove me nuts.

But then I realized—I do the same thing to my kids.

"Turn off the TV and do your homework—now!"

"Time for dinner. Put the game away."

"Close up that book, it's time to practice piano."

Now! This instant!

I know how discouraged I felt when my husband expected me to crawl inside his brain and synchronize my internal clock to his. It was usually when I was in the middle of something else, and I struggled to make a quick mental shift. Over time, we've learned that a simple heads-up helps keep the peace and demonstrates respect for one another.

Likewise, expecting my kids to jump when I say jump—without warning and with no regard for their train of thought or activity—shows a lack of respect for them as individuals. Yes, they're kids and they need to obey authority. But they're also human beings; therefore, they deserve kindness, dignity, and a little bit of space.

So now we harness the power of the five-minute warning. It makes all the difference.

"Sweetie, five more minutes with that game, then it's time to wash up for dinner."

"We're leaving for the library in five minutes. Make sure you have your shoes on."

"Finish your graham crackers, girls. Bedtime is in five minutes."

Warning your children of what's coming next not only exhibits gentleness and respect but also actually empowers them to obey. If you're a stickler for obeying the first time—like I am—then the five-minute warning can create the space your kids need to transition from one activity to the next without being tempted to rebel.

It makes sense, really. Unreasonable or sudden demands are much harder to meet. If you want to set your kids up for success, offer them a five-minute warning. They'll be more likely to cooperate, you'll spare yourself the frustration of barking, and the entire family can actually follow a schedule that works for everyone.

5. Focus on the Positive

Every God-given character trait has a positive and negative side. That's because as fallen humans, anything God created us to use for good can just as easily be used for sinful purposes.

For example, is your child strong-willed? Someday God will use that fierce conviction to serve His kingdom well. Meanwhile, you may face a few green-bean standoffs at the dinner table.

Or maybe your child was blessed with inherent leadership abilities that will one day make a tremendous impact on the business world, church, or family. Until then, though, you'll work hard to curb bossy outbursts.

My parents used to call me their rain cloud because I cried all the time. Today I use my innate sensitivity and spiritual gift of empathy to minister to women in their heartache. I wouldn't want to be anybody else.

Do you see where I'm going with this? Name any trait you wish your child did *not* possess, and flip it around. Discover how it can be channeled toward productive causes. In order to encourage our children to use their abilities for good as they grow and mature into the people God designed them to be, we parents need to see the good within them first—and help them see it, too.

6. Be Their Safe Place

As my kids grow older, I'm learning it's harder to uncover their inmost thoughts. I don't want my daughters to be afraid to talk to

—— Redefine Your Child's —— "Bad" Qualities

Every God-given character trait has a flip side. Often in children we will recognize the untrained, "negative" side of certain characteristics before our kids learn to use them constructively. On this work sheet, write a list of "negative" character traits each child in your family possesses. Then redefine those traits with a positive spin. See this chapter's Let's Dig In! question 7 for examples.

Remember—our job as moms is not to change our children's characteristics, but to teach them to use those characteristics for good and godly purposes!

Child's name: _____

"Bad" Quality	Redefined "Good" Quality

me about anything. But I also want to maintain a level of authority as the grown-up who's due some respect. So I've discovered a solution—a safe place to share raw emotions where nobody gets mad or in trouble. We call it our "feelings notebook."

Here's how it works.

I write a message to my child in a special notebook; she replies in the same notebook, back and forth, back and forth. The feelings notebook has three simple ground rules:

- What's in the notebook stays between us.
- Mom is not allowed to punish for what is revealed in the notebook. I can, however, discuss and guide.

Child's name: _____

"Bad" Quality	Redefined "Good" Quality

Child's name: _____

"Bad" Quality	Redefined "Good" Quality

If you like the feelings notebook idea but your child can't yet read or write, try my helpful work sheet, "Let's Talk About Your Feelings." It can be downloaded from beckykopitzke.com/crankymomfix.

- We cannot use the notebook to insult, harm, or call names. We follow Ephesians 4:29: "Do not let any unwholesome talk come out of your mouths, but only what is helpful for building others up according to their needs, that it may benefit those who listen."

Maybe your child isn't a writer. But will he draw? Read and respond some other way? It could be as simple as offering a color code: draw a red line if you're angry, a blue line if you're sad. Or maybe your child will take well to a texting thread or email. Whatever format you use, the feelings notebook is a springboard from which you can launch merciful conversations. It allows tumultuous young questions and emotions to come tumbling out without fear of condemnation. And it invites children to express themselves in a way that also protects their desire to obey God by honoring their mom and dad.

Let's Dig In!

1. At the start of this chapter, we identified the Bible's priority list for our relationships: God first, then marriage, then children. No singular verse or passage spells this out explicitly, but overall we see this principle explained clearly in Scripture.

First read Deuteronomy 6:5; Colossians 1:16–17; and 1 Corinthians 8:6. Who should we love with all our heart, soul, and strength? Who were we created for? Who do we live for? Clearly God is to be our top priority and our top relationship. He supplies all our needs (Philippians 4:19), gives us strength to get through every day (Philippians 4:13), and He alone can save us (Acts 4:12).

Next read Ephesians 5:25. Christ's first priority was His relationship with God the Father, then came His second priority, the church—meaning, God's people. So a man who loves his wife "as Christ loved the church" puts her next in line to God. Ephesians 5:22 says wives are to love and submit to their husbands "as you do to the Lord." This also means our husbands are second only to God.

And finally, we can place our children third in line. Ephesians 5:31 says a husband and wife become one flesh; therefore, nothing should come between them, including children. That means kids are not supposed to be a greater priority than the marriage between their mom and dad. Yet our calling to raise the next generation of God's followers is vitally important to the kingdom (see Proverbs 22:6 and Ephesians 6:3); therefore, sons and daughters are a parent's third-highest priority. All this is to say—our children are not *most* important (God and marriage come first), but they're still in the top three.

How do your own relationship priorities compare to God's? What steps can you take—even this week—to put God first, then your husband, then your kids?

2. Do you know your child's love language? How can you improve on "speaking" love in ways your child best "hears" or receives love?

3. Revisit Proverbs 22:15: "Folly is bound up in the heart of a child." The second half of that verse talks about discipline, which we'll explore in chapter 12. For now, let's focus on the

"folly" aspect. Has your child ever done something dumb? How did you react at the time? Can you see how your child's natural, age-appropriate foolishness or ignorance played a role in his poor decision? Why is it wise in some cases to teach before we punish? (Again, this does not necessarily apply to an incident involving your child's safety. If he runs into oncoming traffic, by all means, yank him back and bite his head off. *Then* explain why he should never, ever, EVER do that again. Heaven help us all.)

4. Did you ever do something foolish when you were a kid, not with a spirit of rebellion but simply because you didn't know any better? Why did you do it? What were you thinking at the time?

5. Do you tend to treat your children like servants? How can we teach our kids to serve others and work "as working for the Lord" (Colossians 3:23), yet not "provoke or irritate or exasperate" them "[with demands that are trivial or unreasonable or humiliating or abusive]" (Colossians 3:21 AMP)? How does this balance change as our children grow older?

6. How does a five-minute warning actually empower our children to obey?

7. What "negative" characteristics do you observe in your child? Can you identify the positive side of each of these traits? For example, with training and time, each of these "bad" qualities can be channeled for good:

"Bad" Quality	Redefined "Good" Quality
Bossy	Leadership skills
Nosy	Inquisitive
Tattler	Values justice
Shy	Discerning, introspective
Easily distracted	Observant, aware
Overly sensitive	Compassionate
Messy	Creative
Rowdy	Energetic, brave
Stubborn	Passionate, independent

8. Are you intentional about building trust and rapport with your children? Do they see you as a safe place to share their emotions, questions, and vulnerabilities? Recall in the beginning of this chapter we encountered Jesus welcoming children into His presence in Mark 10:13–15. How can we be more like Jesus in this respect? In verse 14 He says, "Let the little children come to me, and do not hinder them." As parents, how can we apply these words to our own homes?

8

This Family Is Now in Session

I once worked for a boss who was extremely fond of team meetings. On an average week, my co-workers and I spent about 70 percent of our time in a boardroom, discussing every detail of the work we had to do. That left only 30 percent of the day to actually *do* the work we had to do.

Overkill? I'd say so.

However, in families, I believe the opposite needs to be true. We spend so much of our time doing the work—prepping meals, studying for exams, driving to sports meets, mowing the lawn— that we rarely sit down together and talk about it all.

What if we looked at our families as business entities, in a sense? We have supervisors (Mom and Dad), team members (kids), interns (babies, toddlers, and possibly dogs). Each role carries certain responsibilities, often with deadlines and budgets attached.

For example, supervisors must feed team members breakfast before the school bus arrives, enroll them in swim lessons before the early bird discount expires, and pay the electric bill on time.

Team members, for their part, must clean their room on Saturday, wash their hands before dinner, finish their broccoli before dessert, and return the car to the garage by curfew.

Even the poor interns must nap at noon and ditch their Pull-Ups before preschool.

All these tasks and more are accomplished in a timely manner so the "company" can thrive. How can we keep track of it all?

Do what the boss would do. Hold a meeting.

Remember, our objective is to bridge the communication gap and discover how best to motivate, train, and love our children—to "meet them where they are." One key solution, then, is to quite literally *meet* them, or shall we say meet *with* them. I call it the family meeting.

What Is a Family Meeting, and Why Do We Need One?

A family meeting is a simple opportunity to get everybody around the table to talk about important family stuff. If you're groaning at the idea, let me assure you it's not meant to be just another obligation—as if we don't have enough to do already. Rather, a family meeting should help make all the other to-do's more efficient and meaningful. Whether you're a natural-born planner or a go-with-the-flow mom, there are several wise reasons to hold a family meeting. Let's explore them one by one.

Family meetings help you slow down. Busyness has become a plague upon families. When we're focused on running from one activity to the next and completing a list of tasks day after day, we can fall into the habit of doing life *with* one another rather than *for* one another. A family meeting is a chance to slow down, gather, pray—and to talk about what's on your heart, not just your agenda. That kind of open communication is vital to building strong, trusting bonds.

Of course, meaningful conversations don't need to be scheduled; ideally we're inviting them often, organically, at all hours as opportunities arise. But when life gets hectic, busyness has a way of squandering our energy and availability for heart-to-heart chats. We neglect to look each other in the eyes. Setting aside time and attention for a family meeting shows our kids that family truly is a priority—not just in theory but in our calendars, too.

Family meetings build solidarity. "We're a team!" If my kids had a dollar for every time I told them that, they could host their own college funds. I'm constantly reminding my children that God brought us Kopitzkes together on purpose, for a purpose; therefore, we need to work together, fight for each other, and cheer each other on. Consider the family meeting like a huddle—a chance to map out the game plan and remind the kids you've got their back.

Family meetings get everybody on the same page. A year ago, my friend Brooke faced a deeply rooted conflict in her marriage. In order to save their family, she and her husband had to undergo some gut-wrenching discussions—which their kids viewed as fighting.

"We realized communication in our family was not good overall, and we wanted to change that," Brooke said. "At first, a family meeting was a way for us to set aside time to tell our sons what was happening. We knew they were nervous about the arguing, and we wanted to assure them we were committed to working things out—that the fighting was actually a sign our marriage was getting stronger because we were finally talking through the hard things."

Soon they added other topics to their meeting plans, including a family devotion, prayer requests, and an open forum for the boys to share what was happening in their lives. Now whether they're tackling issues or celebrating praises, the family meeting provides a precious opportunity to touch base and build healthy communication. "We're unbelievably different from where we were a year ago, and these meetings have been a big part of that," Brooke said. "They've made such a difference in the way we get along."

Family meetings give the kids a voice. Family meetings can give children ownership and show them you respect them as individuals. All you need to do is let them speak up—and allow them to make some decisions.

"At one point my husband and I realized we were talking a lot," Brooke said, "but we really wanted to hear from our kids and understand their hearts—what they were needing, how they were feeling, and why. So we invited them to plan the next meeting."

And did they ever.

Brooke's older son wrote an agenda that included kicking off the meeting with a worship song. Her younger son shared a Bible verse and presented a five-minute sermon on how it related to their lives. The boys played a video clip and invited each family member to share news from work or school. They talked about everything from marriage counseling to video games.

"We're learning to let the kids share what's important to them, even if it doesn't seem like a big deal to us," Brooke said. "When we show respect for what matters to our boys—like video games— it's like they invite us in. We get a better picture of who they are and what motivates them."

The best part? Brooke's kids love the family meeting. "I mean, really," she said, "what teenage boys actually *want* to sit down and talk to their parents? But ours do. The family meeting has become something we all look forward to."

Family meetings affirm family values. Multiple biblical principles are at play when a family gathers to address its collective needs. Consider some of these ways in which a family meeting invites us to put our faith into practice—together.

- Begin and end each meeting with a prayer or devotion to establish God as sovereign over the family.
  "For where two or three gather in my name, there am I with them."—Matthew 18:20
- Take a genuine interest in one another's lives.
  "Do nothing out of selfish ambition or vain conceit. Rather, in humility value others above yourselves, not

looking to your own interests but each of you to the interests of the others."—Philippians 2:3–4

- Speak openly about concerns.

  "Therefore, having put away falsehood, let each one of you speak the truth with his neighbor, for we are members one of another."—Ephesians 4:25 ESV

- Learn to listen.

  "My dear brothers and sisters, take note of this: Everyone should be quick to listen, slow to speak and slow to become angry."—James 1:19

- Resolve conflicts in a God-honoring way.

  "Finally, brothers and sisters, rejoice! Strive for full restoration, encourage one another, be of one mind, live in peace. And the God of love and peace will be with you."—2 Corinthians 13:11

- Extend forgiveness for any hurts.

  "Be kind and compassionate to one another, forgiving each other, just as in Christ God forgave you."—Ephesians 4:32

- Communicate regularly to keep grudges from forming.

  "See to it that no one falls short of the grace of God and that no bitter root grows up to cause trouble and defile many."—Hebrews 12:15

- Share words of encouragement around the table.

  "Therefore encourage one another and build each other up, just as in fact you are doing."—1 Thessalonians 5:11

- Maintain harmony within the household.

  "If it is possible, as far as it depends on you, live at peace with everyone."—Romans 12:18

How to Run a Fabulous Family Meeting

You've gathered everybody around the table. Phones are on silent, the TV is off, and you've managed to peel the kids away from all iPads, earbuds, and Xbox distractions. You've got snacks—go, Mom! You're ready to do this thing! Now what?

Here are six practical guidelines for making the most of your family meeting.

1. Make it fun. Seriously, the last thing you want is to bore the kids to the point of grumbling or daydreaming. What would engage their imaginations, spur a sense of teamwork, and get them giggling—or at least not rolling their eyes, amen? Try incorporating a silly game, a video clip, or a series of jokes for starters. And—for your sanity and theirs—don't forget the food! Serve a special takeout meal, dessert, or favorite appetizer that's reserved only for family meetings. That's not bribery, my friends; it's part of the ambience. The point is to show your family this meeting is a celebration—not a holding cell.

2. Bring your happy face to the table. Grumpy mom, can we chat? Here's the thing. Nobody's going to believe the family meeting is fun if you don't reflect happiness in your own demeanor. By that I mean be real and honest, yes, of course—but please do not use the family meeting as a forum to air only grievances and no praise, nor to badger your husband and kids for everything they've done to irk you. The meeting should be a safe place to share concerns as well as encouragement. Therefore, let's allow the Bible to guide the way we speak and act.

> Kind words are like honey—sweet to the soul and healthy for the body.
>
> Proverbs 16:24 NLT

Remember in chapter 3 we talked about speaking love, not war? This is an important principle to keep in mind during the family meeting, especially when addressing complaints. In every circumstance we have a choice to use our words as handguns or honey. Choose honey. It heals the soul.

> Get rid of all bitterness, rage and anger, brawling and slander, along with every form of malice. Be kind and compassionate to

one another, forgiving each other, just as in Christ God forgave you.

Ephesians 4:31–32

Bitter much? God says eradicate it—which means checking yourself daily for any sign of animosity, resentment or grudge, and handing it over to Him. He knows how to manage your issues far better than your children can.

Be careful not to allow the family meeting to become a gripe session or a gang-up on any one person. Avoid sweeping statements like "you never" or "I always." Refrain from constantly digging up "old business," and instead resolve issues as they arise, then release them to the Lord. Think forward, not behind. Be sensitive to one another and forgive, forgive, forgive.

> Live in harmony with each other. Don't be arrogant, but be friendly to humble people. Don't think that you are smarter than you really are.
>
> Romans 12:16 GW

Sometimes as adults we can easily dismiss our kids' concerns or opinions as childlike and therefore ridiculous. But those concerns are not ridiculous to them. The wise and humble mom will stoop to enter her child's world where she can empathize, understand, and inspire.

3. Get the kids involved. Do you want your kids to get excited about the family meeting? Give them some ownership in the process. Just like Brooke invited her boys to plan their agenda, assigning some portion of the meeting to your kids can boost their enthusiasm *and* show respect for their interests. Maybe it's as simple as letting them choose the snack, or asking for their opinions on agenda items such as where to go on vacation or what to get Grandma for her birthday. Older children can suggest topics to discuss or plan a related family activity. Sometimes we Kopitzkes include an entertainment portion and invite the kids to play a piano song or demonstrate a magic trick. However you do it, getting the children involved will reinforce the fact that the family meeting is a family affair—and everybody has a voice.

4. Stay within the youngest attention span. This can be tricky if you have "interns" (toddlers or younger), but as a general rule, try not to drag the meeting past the youngest child's threshold for giving a rip. If your kids span a wide range of ages, consider meeting during the baby's naptime or offer a special bin of "meeting toys" that your toddler can explore while the older kids talk. Just be sure you're not using the younger kids as an excuse not to meet, nor the older kids as an excuse to force a four-year-old to sit still for an hour. Be prepared to keep all ages and stages occupied according to their needs.

5. Talk about what matters. What's important to your family? What recurring concerns or needs do you face? What special events are coming up? How do you want to live out your faith as a family? The answers to these questions will help you determine what topics to address during your family meetings. Be flexible and willing to test what works and what doesn't. As long as you're discussing what's relevant to you, your husband, and the kids, you're on the right track.

Here are some topics to consider:

- Weekly activity schedules—What's coming up? Who needs to be where? How are you going to juggle multiple calendars?
- Meal plans and shopping lists—Any special requests?
- Extracurricular or summer activities—sports, camps, classes, etc.
- Vacation plans
- School events or upcoming projects
- Academic concerns
- Friendship challenges or updates

- Chore schedules
- Family volunteer projects
- Acts of kindness
- Hurt feelings
- Good news
- Encouragement—Invite everybody to share an encouraging word for each family member!
- Prayer requests

6. Meet regularly. Some families meet monthly, some weekly. It's *your* family meeting, so find what works for you and stick to it. A commitment to the meeting is a commitment to each other—and to the God who designed your family in the first place.

> And let us consider how we may spur one another on toward love and good deeds, not giving up meeting together, as some are in the habit of doing, but encouraging one another—and all the more as you see the Day approaching.
>
> Hebrews 10:24–25

 *Let's Dig In!*

1. Read Romans 12:2. What does it mean to "conform to the pattern of this world"? In what ways does our modern society's emphasis on productivity and busyness conflict with God's values?

2. Now study Mark 6:31; Matthew 11:28–30; Haggai 1:5–9; and Matthew 6:33. Have you been focusing more on your to-do's than on God and His role within your family life? How can a family meeting help your family slow down and prioritize what matters most?

3. Consider the following Bible passages on teamwork: Ecclesiastes 4:9–12; Proverbs 27:17; 1 Corinthians 12:12–26; and Ephesians 4:16. How do the members of your family work together as a team? Do you emphasize unity and teamwork among your core family values? Why or why not?

4. Revisit 2 Corinthians 13:11. Why do you think God wants us to resolve conflicts peaceably? How does conflict affect our family unity? Certainly God doesn't expect every person in a family to have the same personality and preferences; He created each of us unique by design. What, then, does it mean to "be of one mind" as a family? How does encouragement play a role in achieving that goal?

5. Consider James 1:19; Proverbs 18:2; and Proverbs 20:5. Are you a good listener? Are you available for your husband or children when they want to talk? Do you open your ears to understand the heart behind their words? How can you take steps to improve your listening skills for your family this week?

6. Do you truly care about what matters to your kids, or do you view their interests as immature or unimportant? Children live in a child's world. Teens live in a teen's world, and in some ways it might be harsher than ours. Consider how your children's reality is different from yours. How can you be intentional about entering in? How can a family meeting help in that regard?

7. Proverbs 16:24 says "kind words are like honey" (NLT). Back in Bible times, there was no supermarket aisle filled with candy, sacks of sugar, or Stevia packets. Honey was the only reasonably available sweetener, and even then it required contending with bees in order to harvest! With those factors in mind, how "sweet" does the Bible suggest kind words truly are? How can you use yours to encourage your family?

8. How can you get your kids actively involved in planning or participating in your family meeting? Spend some time brainstorming ways the kids might enjoy contributing according to their interests.

Discipline That Works

"When my kids become wild and unruly, I use a nice, safe playpen. When they're finished, I climb out."—Erma Bombeck

9

Jesus Is Not a Killjoy

"Maaaamaaaa!" My younger daughter, age six at the time, screamed and wailed and gasped for air. I stood in the hallway with my ear to her bedroom door.

"Sweetheart, please calm down. If you stop screaming, I will come in." I studied the handmade posters taped to the door. One said, "I am at work—please knock." The other, "No *dinosors* allowed." Precious signs of the sweet child who once lived inside the maniac I was talking to now.

"Maaaamaaaa!" Her sobbing intensified. My heart lurched in my chest because, doggone it, she'd done it to herself. Twenty minutes earlier she'd sassed me in the kitchen and I called her on it. She knew she owed me an apology.

But she refused to give it. Stubborn little bug. Therefore, I had to follow through.

"Go to your room and talk to Jesus," I'd told her.

"Noooo!! I don't WANT to!"

"If you do not apologize, you will lose the privilege of going on our family bike ride. You will have to stay home." *Which means your mother will have to stay home, too, grrrr.* "Please, sweetheart. Make the right choice."

She didn't. Which brought me to the hallway, where after listening to my daughter work herself into a grand tizzy, I attempted once again to sweet talk some sense into her.

"Calm down, my love. I'm right here outside the door."

"Noooo!" More wailing.

"It doesn't have to be this way. Say you're sorry and everything will be fixed."

"No!!!"

"Baby, you're choosing this tantrum. Just do the right thing, and I can open the door."

I will set you free.

Hmmm. Who does that sound like?

> Those whom I love I rebuke and discipline. So be earnest and repent. Here I am! I stand at the door and knock. If anyone hears my voice and opens the door, I will come in and eat with that person, and they with me. To the one who is victorious, I will give the right to sit with me on my throne, just as I was victorious and sat down with my Father on his throne.
>
> Revelation 3:19–21

We're all stubborn, really. We want what we want, and we hate it when God has other ideas. So sometimes we fight and kick and refuse to give in. We grab hold of our mistakes or our bad choices and wrap them around us like a shield from God's grace. Because hey, accepting grace is like admitting defeat, right? It's like acknowledging we were wrong in the first place. So we'd rather suffer. We'd rather stand in our bedrooms howling and missing out on the proverbial bike ride.

But the Lord is standing just inches away, separated only by the door of our own stinking pride. He's pleading, *Please, child, do the right thing. This will not go well for you if you don't. Trust me. Let me guide you. You just need to be willing to break a little—and I will be right here, ready to patch you back up.*

God is such a loving parent. I want to be like Him. Don't you?

We've just spent half this book exploring how a mom's own issues can get in the way of parenting kindly. We've discussed opportunities to choose gentleness and build trust and rapport. We've tucked the tools in our belts that can help us manage and even prevent scenarios like my daughter's—when the kids throw fits, disobey, talk back, bicker, beg, and whine. Yet the truth is, our risk management can only go so far. Children are individuals with minds of their own. And just like we moms sometimes fall prey to crankiness, so do our sons and daughters. That's when our job is to discipline.

Ugh. *Discipline.* Just saying the word makes my stomach hurt. Nobody likes discipline, whether you're the giver or the getter. Even the Bible agrees, "No discipline seems pleasant at the time, but painful" (Hebrews 12:11). Yet discipline is most definitely a necessary and biblical part of the parenting process. Because, as the rest of verse 11 says, "Later on, however, it produces a harvest of righteousness and peace for those who have been trained by it."

Do you believe discipline can be delivered with patience, gentleness, and love? It can. Discipline—punishment, consequences, correction, whatever you choose to call it—is a normal part of raising our children with intention and grace. *How* we do it, though, marks the difference between a cranky mom and a kind one.

In these next four chapters we're going to explore some key principles and strategies for discipline that works—without selling your soul to the dark side.

What Kind of God Do You Serve?

A few years ago my husband installed a GPS in our minivan because, silly us, we thought it would be helpful. Turns out it only got me in trouble.

"Mom, you're going over the speed limit." My older daughter piped up from the back seat. She was seven years old back then, compliant and smart. I glanced at the GPS, that know-it-all black nark box suctioned to the dashboard. Hmph.

Speed Limit: 30 / MPH: 37

"Actually, the speed limit here is 35, sweetheart. The GPS is wrong."

"But, Mom, 37 is still two more than 35."

Yep. Sometimes advanced math skills are not an attractive quality in children. But rather than lecture my daughter on the nuances of speed limit enforcement, I decided to humble myself and encourage her obedience.

"You're right, lovey. Thank you for pointing out my mistake. I'll slow down." And then we crept the rest of our route to school, while other vehicles passed us on both sides.

Ever since my daughter began scrutinizing my driving, I now climb behind the wheel in trepidation, as if a squad car is trailing me everywhere I go, eager to pounce with a ticket and three points on my license. This might make me pay closer attention to my speed, but it's really no way to live. I'm just waiting for the billy club to come down on my head at any moment.

Do you ever see God that way?

Like He's some stern, cosmic traffic cop with tickets in hand and a quota to fill. He watches your every move, hungry to nail you for any minor—or major—offense. So you keep your eyes on the rearview mirror and travel cautiously, anxiously through life. As if God gets His kicks out of punishing you.

Really?

I used to think that, too.

But let's meet the God of the Bible.

The Lord is compassionate and merciful, slow to get angry and filled with unfailing love. He will not constantly accuse us, nor remain angry forever. He does not punish us for all our sins; he does not deal harshly with us, as we deserve. For his unfailing love toward those who fear him is as great as the height of the heavens above the earth.

Psalm 103:8–11 NLT

I think it's hard to imagine God as He really is—compassionate and overwhelmingly forgiving—because we don't actually know many *people* like that. People complain. People find fault with each other. People hold grudges and keep score. Even the "nice" people struggle to forgive "bad" offenses.

God doesn't.

He isn't like us.

His ways are not our ways. His thoughts are not our thoughts (Isaiah 55:8–9).

He is eternally trustworthy (Proverbs 3:5–6);

. . . always good (Psalm 107:1);

. . . and never changing (Hebrews 13:8).

He doesn't keep a record of our mistakes (1 Corinthians 13:5).

He loves us in spite of them (John 3:16; 1 John 3:1).

Isn't that good news?

So if your picture of God doesn't match the picture painted in the Bible, it's time to toss your old assumptions and dig into the book. Get ready to encounter an amazing God—the One who loves us like crazy and forgives us beyond measure. He does not shame us. He does not condemn us. He restores us and guides us—even when we happen to drive a couple miles over the speed limit, or worse.

Why am I telling you all this? Because if we don't know the real God, we cannot teach Him to our children. And our kids need to know they belong to a gracious, compassionate, unwavering Father. He is not mean. He is not vindictive. He does not ignore them or abandon them or take interest in them only when moved to punish. God exists within their joys and victories, too.

Is your parenting reflecting that truth?

I want to share with you now a crucial parenting rule for Christian families. Read it, memorize it, post it on your bathroom mirror—do whatever you have to do to drill this very important principle into your momma head.

Do not make Jesus a killjoy.

We need to bring the Lord into every situation—happy, mad, sad, fun, all of it. Because if we mention the things of God only in times of scolding, our kids will see Him as the bad cop, the cruel judge, the party pooper—rather than a loving and supportive Father who is actively involved in every aspect of their lives.

Hammer Words vs. Paintbrush Words

I'm a huge advocate for drawing on God's Word to train our kids. The Bible makes it clear: "All Scripture is God-breathed and is useful for teaching, rebuking, correcting and training in righteousness, so that the servant of God may be thoroughly equipped for every good work" (2 Timothy 3:16–17). Amen! The Bible is our source of wisdom—yes, by all means, let's apply it to our children's lives!

In doing so, though, we need to ensure we're using Scripture not just to convict but also to equip and encourage. Think of it as the difference between a hammer and a paintbrush. One pounds holes in the wall; the other transforms it.

Hammer words sound like this.

Don't you walk away when I'm talking to you! God says obey your parents! (Colossians 3:20).
You shouldn't have lied to me. God detests lying lips (Proverbs 12:22).
Do your chores and quit grumbling, because the Bible says you should do everything without complaining (Philippians 2:14).

Parents who use hammer words to discipline have the right idea, if not always the right delivery. Yes, our children need to recognize sin as sin, and the Bible has plenty of verses to help nail them on their faults. However, is that our only goal? To tell the kids they're wrong, naughty, disappointing?

No.

Our true end goal should be to show them the better choice (which is positive, God-honoring behavior) and equip them to grasp it. This requires approaching every infraction as an opportunity to train our children toward godly character—to build them up rather than tear them down (Proverbs 14:1).

How can we do this?

It's simple.

Label the bad behavior. Then combat it with the *opposite* truths in Scripture. I call these paintbrush words.

For example—let's say your son picks a fight with his brother. That's called quarreling. You might be tempted to spout off Bible verses (hammer words) about why they should *not* quarrel, such as, "Anyone who is angry with a brother or sister will be subject to judgment" (Matthew 5:22).

Okay. But what does that teach your child besides that he's in big, fat trouble?

Let's go one step further and teach him why he should do the opposite of quarreling—which is to live in peace. Love. Harmony. The Bible is filled with verses on that sort of thing.

Hey, buddy, I think you need to let the peace of Christ start ruling in your heart. God called you to live in peace with your brother (Colossians 3:15).

Did you know kindness and peace are fruit of the Spirit? (Galatians 5:22). That means you have a choice to behave that way instead of fighting. Wouldn't you rather be getting along with your brother right now?

I can tell something is really bothering you, and you're taking it out on your brother. Go to your room for a while to calm down, and talk to Jesus because He says you can "cast all your anxiety on him because he cares for you" (1 Peter 5:7).

Yes, in the midst of tantrums or heated rebellion, our children may need a firm hand to guide them. Even Jesus sometimes scolded His disciples for their selfishness or dim wits. Imagine the pit in

Paintbrush Words

Here are some helpful Bible verses to apply in a variety of parenting situations.

Bickering

Opposite theme in Scripture: harmony

Romans 12:16–18
Romans 14:19
I Peter 3:8–11
I Peter 4:8
Galatians 6:10
Colossians 3:14
I Corinthians 1:10

Disobedience

Opposite theme in Scripture: obedience

I John 5:3
Colossians 3:20
Hebrews 4:15
James 1:22–25
I Corinthians 10:13
Galatians 6:9

Defiance

Opposite theme in Scripture: respect for authority

Romans 13:1
Proverbs 6:20
Ephesians 6:1–3
Titus 3:1–3
I Peter 2:13–14
Hebrews 13:17
I Peter 5:5

Complaining/Ingratitude

Opposite theme in Scripture: gratitude

I Thessalonians 5:16–18
Colossians 3:17
Philippians 4:8
Psalm 106:1

Jealousy

Opposite theme in Scripture: sympathetic joy, serving others

I Corinthians 13:4
Galatians 5:14
I Thessalonians 5:11
I Peter 4:10
Romans 12:15

Greed

Opposite theme in Scripture: generosity

Proverbs 11:25
Proverbs 16:8
Proverbs 22:9
Psalm 112:5
Matthew 6:19–21
Matthew 6:33
Luke 6:38
2 Corinthians 9:6

Discontentment

Opposite theme in Scripture: contentment

Isaiah 26:3
Philippians 4:12–13
Psalm 84:11
I Timothy 6:6–7
Psalm 37:4

Bragging

Opposite theme in Scripture: humility

Colossians 3:12
Ephesians 4:2
James 4:6
James 4:10
Luke 14:11
Micah 6:8
Proverbs 22:4
Psalm 25:9

Dishonesty

Opposite theme in Scripture: honesty, integrity

2 Corinthians 8:21
2 Timothy 2:15
Ephesians 4:25
Proverbs 10:9
Proverbs 11:3
Proverbs 12:22

Mistreating others
Opposite theme in Scripture: kindness, love

Luke 6:31
Mark 12:31
James 3:17
Ephesians 4:32
1 John 3:18
Philippians 4:8–9
1 Corinthians 13:1–7
Colossians 3:12

Selfishness
Opposite theme in Scripture: selflessness, generosity

Philippians 2:3–4
Romans 12:10
1 Corinthians 13:4–6
Galatians 6:2
Romans 15:1–3
Hebrews 13:16
Acts 20:35
John 3:16
2 Corinthians 8:9

Teasing/name calling
Opposite theme in Scripture: speaking kind and encouraging words

Ephesians 4:29
Colossians 4:6
Psalm 141:3

Proverbs 16:24
Proverbs 15:1–2, 4
Proverbs 21:23
Proverbs 31:26
Proverbs 17:27
Proverbs 12:18
Titus 3:2

Worry/fear/anxiety
Opposite theme in Scripture: trust, courage, peace

Joshua 1:9
Isaiah 41:10
2 Timothy 1:7
John 14:27
Philippians 4:6–7
2 Thessalonians 3:16
Psalm 55:22
Psalm 23:4
Psalm 27:1
Psalm 56:3–4
1 Peter 5:7
Proverbs 3:5–6
Matthew 6:25–34
Romans 8:38–39

Poor self-worth
Opposite theme in Scripture: God treasures you!

Psalm 139:13–14
Romans 5:8
John 1:12
2 Corinthians 5:17
1 Corinthians 6:19–20

Romans 8:1
Ephesians 1:4–6
Ephesians 2:10
1 John 3:1
Zephaniah 3:17

Laziness
Opposite theme in Scripture: hard work

Genesis 2:15
Colossians 3:17
Colossians 3:23
Psalm 90:17
Philippians 4:13
1 Thessalonians 4:11–12
Proverbs 12:11
Proverbs 16:3
Matthew 5:16
1 Corinthians 15:58

Friendship trouble
Opposite theme in Scripture: choose good friends, be a good friend

Luke 6:31
Proverbs 12:26
Proverbs 13:20
Proverbs 17:17
Proverbs 27:17
Colossians 3:12–14

Peter's stomach when Jesus told him, "Get away from me, Satan!" Yikes. God isn't one to sugarcoat anything.

Yet He is also kind and forgiving. He is compassionate, wise, and welcoming. God cares more about our hearts than our actions—because He knows one is rooted in the other.

> Above all else, guard your heart, for everything you do flows from it.
>
> Proverbs 4:23

So let's not just scold our kids for doing wrong. Let's cover their hearts with as many paintbrush words as possible so they can learn to do *right*. Only then can we show them the full picture of who God really is.

Jesus Every Day

What about those times when our children are behaving well? When they're making wise choices, acting loving, achieving milestones, and working hard? Or what about situations in which our kids are struggling through no mistakes of their own and simply need our encouragement and advice? How do paintbrush words impact them then?

Ah. That's the beauty of using Scripture in all situations. It invites Jesus into our everyday moments—and shows the kids that God is *for* them, not against them.

In those cases, paintbrush words look like this.

> *I am so proud of all the hard work and planning you put into your science project. Did you know the Bible says those who work hard will prosper (Proverbs 13:4)? You're putting your faith into action when you focus on your schoolwork. Well done.*
>
> *Thank you for sharing your gum with your brother. God is happy when we share (Hebrews 13:16). It says so right in the Bible!*

> *I know it's been hard making new friends this year. Just re-*
> *member you are wonderfully made (Psalm 139:14). God*
> *created you with an amazing personality. He thinks you're*
> *awesome, and so do I.*

We have so many opportunities throughout the day to affirm our kids with Scripture. All we need to do is open our eyes to the scenery and choose to paint it with God's flawless Word.

For the Mom Who Wants to Set this Book on Fire Right Now

I imagine some of you at this point are thinking, *That's great, Becky, but what if I don't know the Bible very well? How can I use Scripture to train my kids if I don't have any Scripture in my head?*

I hear you. Please don't give up! I've known many fellow moms in your shoes over the years, and my answer is always this: Start.

Just start somewhere, with a few key verses that can help guide you and your kids. Get involved in a Bible study or ask your church if they can connect you with a mentor. If your kids attend a Bible-based club like AWANA, learn the verses right along with them. Read your Bible regularly and highlight portions that strike you or that apply to the lessons you want to teach. Write verses on note cards. Memorize them. Do what works best for you to tuck those words in your heart so that when the need arises, you'll be ready to wield God's Word with gentleness and intention.

You may not think you know much today. But you're reading this book. That in itself is a start! Pick out some of the Bible verses offered throughout these pages and ask God and godly mentors to help you understand how to apply them to your life, your parenting, your relationship with your kids. God wants to give us His discernment! It blesses Him when we ask for it.

If any of you lacks wisdom, you should ask God, who gives generously to all without finding fault, and it will be given to you.

James 1:5

If you keep taking these small steps day after day, before long you'll be surprised how much Bible knowledge you've retained. It will start to spill out of your heart as naturally as breathing—because when we immerse ourselves in God's truth, it becomes a part of how we think, act, and speak.

Let the message about Christ, in all its richness, fill your lives. Teach and counsel each other with all the wisdom he gives. Sing psalms and hymns and spiritual songs to God with thankful hearts.

Colossians 3:16 NLT

Google It

One advantage we have over moms of previous generations is a handy little tool called the Internet. You want to know what God's Word has to say about any particular topic? Google it. For real—just type in "Bible verses about {topic}" or "What does the Bible say about {topic}" and you'll get an endless list of resources. Here are some trusted sites I recommend.

Bible Gateway (biblegateway.com)
Bible Hub (biblehub.com)
Bible Study Tools (biblestudytools.com)
Open Bible (openbible.info)
Crosswalk (crosswalk.com)
Got Questions (gotquestions.org)
The Gospel Coalition (thegospelcoalition.org)
Daily Verses (dailyverses.net)
Desiring God—John Piper (desiringgod.org)
Grace to You—John MacArthur (gty.org)

I know how you feel, sweet mom. I was new to the Bible once, too, and I still have far to go. That's the Christian life. We're never done learning. God's wisdom is a deep well, and we get to draw from it day by day, hour by hour—a true privilege, not a chore. Let's show our kids by example just how awesome God really is. Amen?

Let's Dig In!

1. Do you view God as a benevolent Father, a vindictive traffic cop, or something in between? Why?

2. In the Old Testament, God is often described as mighty, just, and jealous for His glory. He is "a consuming fire" (Deuteronomy 4:24) who "does not leave the guilty unpunished" (Exodus 34:7). This can seem intimidating—but remember, God's wrath is upon those who oppose Him. For the Christian saved by faith, we are "reconciled to [God] through the death of his Son" (Romans 5:10). That means we no longer oppose God; we are His children. He's on our side. Read Romans 8:38–39. How much does God love you?

3. Now read Romans 15:13; 1 Peter 1:8; and Philippians 4:4. According to these Scriptures, knowing and loving Jesus should fill us with what? Fear? Boredom? Dread? No! The answer is *joy*. As believers, we are meant to experience joy in following Christ. Are you allowing God to be a joy in your home, or are you making Him a killjoy?

4. In chapter 7, we discussed Proverbs 22:15, which says "folly is bound up in the heart of a child." Another word for *folly* is *foolishness*. The Hebrew meaning of a fool is one who is without wisdom. Recall from chapter 1 that the source of true

wisdom is God and His Word. Our primary job as parents is to point our children to Him. How are you doing in this area? Are you more likely to use hammer words or paintbrush words?

5. According to Ephesians 6:4, we can correct our children's natural folly and impart wisdom by "bringing them up in the training and instruction of the Lord." Deuteronomy 6:4–9 gives us a visual for what this looks like in our homes. In today's world it might involve this:

- Talk about God throughout the day, pointing to Him in your everyday scenery and routines. This can be as simple as saying, "Look at the sunset God painted for us tonight!" or "I'm so glad God made that sled hill!"
- Display reminders throughout your house. Consider writing verses on a chalkboard, incorporating crosses or Scripture into your home décor, or wearing clothing and jewelry printed with Bible truth.
- Play Christian music at home. Watch Christian movies and TV shows.
- Read the Bible together. Do daily or weekly family devotions.
- Hold fun challenges (with prizes!) for Scripture memorization, or put a quarter in a jar each time your child uses a Bible verse in conversation.

What other ideas do you have for making God's Word a part of your household?

6. In the days of the early church, slave labor was common. Many slaves were treated horribly, but some were trusted helpers in the household. In modern terms, biblical principles concerning slaves and masters can be applied to the employee/boss relationship and, in many ways, to the child/parent relationship as well. Essentially the "master" is someone in a position of authority over the "slave."

With that in mind, read Ephesians 6:5–9 and Colossians 4:1. Although we moms do have authority over our children, how are we to handle that authority?

7. *The Message* paraphrase of Ephesians 6:9 says to masters (i.e., moms), "No abuse, please, and no threats. You and your servants are both under the same Master in heaven. He makes no distinction between you and them."

    Our children are just as precious to God as we are. Therefore, we ought to respect them as fellow humans designed by a holy, flawless heavenly Father—whose perfect Word is meant not just to pierce hearts but to heal and transform them. In what ways might you be abusing your authority?

8. Consider Colossians 3:16: "Let the message of Christ dwell among you richly as you teach and admonish one another with all wisdom . . ." The Greek root for *admonish* is *noutheteó*, which means not necessarily to chastise but to urge.[1]

    Are you urging your kids gently and cheerfully to follow God? As parents we have a daily opportunity to "spur [our children] on toward love and good deeds" (Hebrews 10:24). Let's do that by making it clear that Jesus is not a killjoy. He's the life of the party.

10

Mind, Will, Heart

When my younger daughter was in preschool, she developed a fear of the dark. Every night, on top of coaxing our kiddos to brush their teeth and climb under the covers by the appointed hour, my husband and I now battled shadows and scary noises and murderous bears supposedly hiding in the closet. Our little one would repeatedly patter out of her room past bedtime to ask for another hug, a kiss on the hand, or just a few more minutes to snuggle with Mommy.

On a good night this might have been somewhat endearing. On a cranky night, however, it was just plain maddening. By the time eight o'clock rolled around, my energy evaporated and I wanted nothing more than to flop on the couch with a decent novel and a dim sofa lamp. Unlike some other people in the house, I wasn't the least bit intimidated by dark silence. When are these kids going to understand sleep is a gift??

"Mommy, I'm scared. Can I be with you?"

And there she would appear, her nose peeking over my book cover, her sleepy eyes pleading. I'd look at that sweet face and realize I had a choice. Should I respond according to my feelings? Or according to my knowledge?

One says, I'm tired and cranky. The other says, she's scared.

One says, me me me. The other says, her. Think about her.

One is selfish. The other, sympathetic.

Ironic, isn't it, that knowledge—rather than feelings—can employ sympathy?

Whenever we're faced with a child's wrongdoing, we must all make the choice between how we feel and what we know. The question is—can you tell the difference?

It's time for us to discover one of the most enlightening and empowering tools in the Cranky Mom Fix. I call it the "mind-will-heart" connection. And it's a game changer.

What's at the Root of Your Child's Behavior?

Children disobey sometimes. That's a fact of life. But *why* do they disobey? Is it because they want to make their mother's life miserable? We might feel that way sometimes, but the truth is more complex. As parents we need to unearth the *why* behind the *what* in order to respond with love.

Several years ago I led a Bible study at my church called *Entrusted with a Child's Heart* by Betsy Corning. One of the takeaways I gained from that book is the core idea that a child's behavior is usually rooted in one of three things: the mind, the will, or the heart (emotions).[1] And—here's the essential part— our response should depend on which of the three we're dealing with.

> **Mind—what your child knows.** Have you clearly explained your rules and expectations? Does your child understand them? Is he aware he's breaking a rule?
>
> **Will—what your child chooses.** Does your child understand the rules yet deliberately broke one anyway?

Heart—what your child feels. Is there some underlying emotion or issue affecting your child's mind or will?

Let's use my daughter's fear of the dark as an example.
Mind—Did she know she was expected to stay in her room past lights-out? Yes.
Will—Did she deliberately leave her room anyway? Yes.
If I stopped there, I could conclude my daughter was being naughty and punish her for it. But punishment at that point would not have fixed the problem. In fact, it might have made it worse, because underneath her behavior was an emotional issue: She was afraid.

> Emotion deals with how [children] are handling a situation. They know what to do but they are discouraged or fearful. Their emotions can make them question what they know they should do in a situation. . . . We do not discipline the discouraged child. This child needs to have his heart refocused to trust the Lord. Discipline would only further dishearten the child. As you can see, we cannot ignore mind, will, or emotion in our daily interactions with our children. Basing our responses and actions on their "heart" status will immediately make a difference in how we train and discipline our children.
>
> Betsy Corning, *Entrusted with a Child's Heart* [2]

— If Your Child Is Afraid of the Dark —

Genesis tells us that God created the light and the dark, and He called them both good (Genesis 1:3–5, 31). From an early age, our children can understand this simple truth. We don't need to be afraid of the dark because God made it, He says it's a good thing, and He is watching over us.

Next time your child acts out, quickly assess the mind-will-heart connection. Sometimes misbehavior is simply a matter of not knowing better (mind), which, you'll recall from chapter 7, usually means we need to teach rather than punish. And sometimes their choices are deliberate rebellion (will), which calls for firm consequences. But anytime we can answer "yes" to the heart question, we must address the emotion first—before we move on to discipline.

Check Your Heart

"Mom, do you know what my teacher told us yesterday about George Washington?" My older daughter, in third grade at the time, piped up from the back seat as I shifted into reverse, ready to back the minivan out of the garage.

"I do!" I replied, but then suddenly my kindergartner gasped.

"Mom! Did you bring my dinosaur book??"

Oops. I did promise I'd carry the book since her hands were full of other school gear when we walked out the door. "Hold that thought," I told my older daughter as I shifted back into park, ran inside the house to grab the book, then settled again in the driver's seat.

"Okay, lovey, now tell me, what's the news about George Washington?"

"Grrr . . . Now I forgot what I was going to say!" She snarled into the rearview mirror. "All because of the stupid dinosaur book!"

Whoa. Hold on a second. Violation flags came flying at me from all directions. First of all, we do not allow the word *stupid* in our house (or in the minivan)—and my daughter knows that. Second, little sister was not trying to ruin a conversation; she was saving her forgetful mother from having to backtrack all the way home ten minutes later because one way or another, that book had to make it to school. It was *dinosaur week* in kindergarten, people. Important stuff. And third, what's with the sudden attitude?

I could've reprimanded my daughter for multiple offenses at that moment. But instead, I said this: "Check your heart."

> Above all else, guard your heart, for everything you do flows from it.
>
> Proverbs 4:23

Check your heart—three simple words that carry a powerful message. I talk to my kids often about what's happening inside their hearts—what they're feeling and focusing on—because I want them to realize how their feelings affect their actions, which then affect the people around them. And with Jesus living in their hearts, they can make a choice—to let their feelings boss them around, or to clean out the junk that's causing the nasty behavior.

So when Mom tells them "check your heart," they know that means they need to stop and talk with Jesus. I want them to ask Him—*Right now, Jesus, is my heart holding . . .*

Selfishness?

"Do to others as you would have them do to you" (Luke 6:31).

Unkindness?

"Be kind and compassionate to one another, forgiving each other, just as in Christ God forgave you" (Ephesians 4:32).

Love (or lack of it)?

"And over all these virtues put on love, which binds them all together in perfect unity" (Colossians 3:14).

Maybe in your family the checkpoints will be different. While for my kids the root of bickering usually lies in selfishness or forgetting we're on the same team, for yours maybe it's pride, anger, worry, or some other crud. Customize your heart-checks according to your child's needs—like my friend Jamie did.

I heard my six-year-old daughter yelling at her three-year-old sister. Lots of angry and hurtful words were coming out of her mouth. She's usually quite a cheerful girl, but I had been noticing her becoming more angry and impatient lately. My instinct was to grab her and start yelling at her for being so mean to her sister.

144

But instead, I said, "You have a lot of anger in your heart! Why is your heart so angry?" She burst into tears and told me that her best friend at school had been yelling at her and telling her she wasn't her friend. It turns out the anger wasn't about her sister at all, but about a hurtful friendship situation at school. So we talked about what she could say to her friend next time and had some sweet snuggle and hug time. I'm so grateful I stopped to help her examine her heart before I reacted with even more anger than she was already struggling with. What could have been a hurtful situation became a healing opportunity instead.

How can you help your children check their hearts? This important step not only trains them to recognize their sin and hurt, it also empowers them to conquer it—all without Mom or Dad having to tear into every detail of the wrongdoing.

About that Thing They Call Patience

For me, discovering the mind-will-heart connection was like assembling a jigsaw puzzle. Suddenly all the pieces came together and I could see the full picture of my children's behavior and choices. Such a powerful revelation! Do you see it, too? It all makes sense now, right? Our kids aren't hopeless criminals; they're just ignorant, stubborn, or oversensitive—praise the Lord! *That* we can deal with.

Except.

One piece of the puzzle is still missing. And it doesn't belong to our kids; this one belongs to us, the parents. Trouble is—most of us keep losing it.

Patience.

> But the Holy Spirit produces this kind of fruit in our lives: love, joy, peace, *patience*, kindness, goodness, faithfulness, gentleness, and self-control. . . .
>
> Galatians 5:22–23 NLT (emphasis added)

Patience is a required tool if we hope to discern the root of our children's behavior and then guide them through it peaceably. The Bible says patience comes from the Holy Spirit, which means we Christian moms ought to possess it or at least have access to it if we dig really deep.

Unfortunately, I keep dropping mine under the table, and last week I think the dog ate it.

I mean, come *on*, cranky mother friends. If any woman actually does possess this elusive patience thing, then she must be some freak of human nature who never had a child stick a pretzel up his nose or unwrap a whole box of pantiliners to use for doll diapers. Oh, and apparently "patience" means you don't shoot fire out of your eyeballs when these things happen. I repeat—fire-breathing is NOT a good demonstration of patience.

Neither is barking at your kids to get out the door on time because you're running five minutes late yourself.

Patience is not heaving an annoyed sigh every time your daughter has the audacity to ask for a cup of water—or a hug.

It's not ripping your eyelashes out whenever the kiddos bicker over the same goofy toy—or buying a second one just to save your own soul.

And it's definitely not writing a mental grocery list while your precious child sounds out the word "to-mor-row" in her early reader paperback for the fiftieth time, causing you to wish you'd homeschooled this year so you could've axed reading from the curriculum altogether.

That's not patience. That's normal life.

Sad, don't you think?

I want more patience. Of course I do. But for the love of peace and sanity, ladies, let's not *pray* for it. That's just begging God to give us more unexpected opportunities to practice.

You want patience, my child? I'll help you get it. Here—have a week of the stomach flu. Barf bowls are one of my finest instruments for helping you develop patience. Have fun! I love you!

So what's a mom to do?

What I always do when I'm looking for answers—dig into the Word. And here's what I found.

> We can rejoice, too, when we run into problems and trials, for we know that they are good for us—they help us learn to be patient. And patience develops strength of character in us and helps us trust God more each time we use it until finally our hope and faith are strong and steady.
>
> Romans 5:3–4 TLB

> You need to keep on patiently doing God's will if you want him to do for you all that he has promised.
>
> Hebrews 10:36 TLB

> Since we have such a huge crowd of men of faith watching us from the grandstands, let us strip off anything that slows us down or holds us back, and especially those sins that wrap themselves so tightly around our feet and trip us up; and let us run with patience the particular race that God has set before us.
>
> Hebrews 12:1 TLB

In the Bible, the word *patience* is often synonymous or coupled with the word *endurance*. We tend to think of patience as a gentle, passive state of mind, but is it really? Because to endure doesn't mean just to wait but to *act*—to press on through challenges and pain, to not give up, to fight for the prize.

Therefore, it seems to me, patience is not something we can get.

It's something we forge.

Little by little. Day by day. Hour by hour.

Think of it like fitness training. Don't you wish we could just wake up one day with rippling abs? But no. If a gal wants to get in shape, she has to sweat. She has to push out a few more reps each day until those flabby muscles gain elasticity and strength. She has to *endure*.

We have to endure.

What does that look like?

I think it's a choice. Minute by minute.

A choice not to roll our eyes but to look our children *in the eyes*—even as they're begging for another marshmallow.

A choice to breathe deep and break up the sibling fight without spewing words more hurtful than the ones they just said to each other.

A choice to look at the kitchen mess after a long, exhausting day and opt not to bark or complain or run away—but instead close our eyes for a moment, right there in the kitchen, and pray and thank God for these people who share our homes and our hearts and our personal space. Let's ask Him to help us see them for what they are.

A blessing.

Is it easy? Absolutely not. Some days I still stink at it, personally. And yet, I so desperately want to love my family well. I want to honor God with the way I treat them. I want to protect my own heart from harboring evil even as I'm telling my children to check theirs. Don't you? Patience—*elusive, mysterious patience!*—is at the very core of that desire. It's high time we tackle it.

I can't promise I'll do it perfectly, and chances are you won't either. But perfection isn't what we're going for here. It never is. God's grace will see us through our slip-ups. The goal is to put one foot in front of the other, respond differently today than we did yesterday, until after a week or a month or a year we'll see we've developed a string of patient moments that soon define our character. And our kids will benefit.

And praise God, so will we.

Then, when that happens, we are able to hold our heads high no matter what happens and know that all is well, for we know how dearly God loves us, and we feel this warm love everywhere within us because God has given us the Holy Spirit to fill our hearts with his love.

Romans 5:5 TLB

Let's Dig In!

1. Why should we train our kids to obey? Why does it matter? What does it mean? See John 14:15. We obey because we love and revere God. Are you modeling this for your kids? As moms we have a tremendous responsibility (*opportunity!*) to show our kids how to love and revere God by example. They will pay more attention to our actions than our words. Pray for God to help you shine the light of Christ on your children.

2. Do your kids obey out of love for God, or are they motivated by fear of punishment? Are you showing them how big and amazing and good God is, or is their view of God limited by your own? Children must know they are accepted and secure even when they misbehave. Why? Because that's the kind of love God has for us. And it's what motivates us to gratitude and obedience. See 1 John 4:18–19; Romans 5:8; Romans 8:38–39; and 1 John 1:9.

3. Read Proverbs 4:23. What does the Bible admonish us to guard above all else? Why? In the original Hebrew, the root word for *heart* is *leb*, which means "inner man, mind, will, heart."[3] Isn't that interesting? We've discussed throughout this chapter how a child's behavior is usually rooted in one of three things: mind, will, heart. Yet when the Bible refers to heart, it encompasses all three of those factors together. This is indeed affirmation that, as Proverbs 4:23 says, everything we do "flows from the heart." It's all interconnected. That is why we must not neglect to address a child's heart when applying discipline and training of all kinds.

4. The word *heart* or *leb* appears in Scripture hundreds of times. See Proverbs 27:19; Matthew 6:21; 1 Samuel 16:7; Proverbs

3:5–6; and Psalm 51:10. What do these verses tell you about the importance of the heart in our Christian walk? What can you do this week to fuel your child's heart?

5. When we tell children to "check your heart," we're teaching them to examine the root of their behavior and choices. What's happening inside their hearts to trigger their actions? Here is some of the common junk our hearts can harbor:

- Selfishness (Luke 6:31)
- Anger (Ephesians 4:26–27)
- Unkindness (Ephesians 4:23)
- Lack of love (John 13:34)
- Pride (Romans 12:16)
- Rivalry (Philippians 2:3)
- Worry (Philippians 4:6–7; 1 Peter 5:7)
- Greed (Luke 12:15)

Read Psalm 139:23–24. Take some time today to check your *own* heart. Pray through each of the Scriptures listed above, and ask God to reveal any blind spots in your own behavior and attitude.

6. Do you consider yourself a patient person? Why is patience a necessary ingredient in kinder, gentler parenting? How is it connected to every aspect we've explored so far—from taming the Momster, to communicating more effectively with our kids, to discerning the right approach to misbehavior?

7. Consider our discovery that patience is not something we obtain; it's something we forge. Does this encourage you or discourage you? Why?

8. As moms we may sometimes forget we're not just the parent; we're a child, too—of God's. In what ways does your own heart cause you to step outside of God's expectations for your life? Can you make the mind-will-heart connection

within yourself and pray for the Lord to help heal any emotional issues that tempt you to fight against His will? Consider asking your husband or a close friend to help you examine your own motives and hold you accountable to God's truth.

11

Three Family Rules

Don't hit. Don't kick. Don't bite.

Don't interrupt. Don't yell at your mother. No calling your sister a poophead.

Pick up your toys, don't leave your shoes in the hallway, and finish your homework before anybody even thinks about watching another episode of *Odd Squad*—and I really mean it this time.

Rules. Every household needs them. As soon as the baby learns to spit out peas, we parents learn to say "no!" Rules are a natural part of training and protecting our children.

But they can get a little out of hand.

Early in our parenting career, my husband and I established new rules according to whatever latest boundaries our children discovered and tested. They leapt off the sofa; we said *no jumping on the furniture.* They begged for Popsicles; we explained *no treats for breakfast.* They disagreed with bedtime; we said *no reading after lights-out.*

Eventually we had so many rules that our kids couldn't remember them all—and neither could we.

Until one day we discovered the three-rule system. And it changed our lives.

Three Family Rules—Yes, Only Three

In my first eight years of parenting, I tried several different systems for training and discipline. Charts, rewards, stickers, tickets, you name it. Some solutions worked and some didn't, but none of them stuck for long. So when my friend Jedotta told me about her three family rules, I was intrigued. Really? Only three rules? That's it?

Yes. And the system is not only brilliant, it works.

Jedotta learned the three-rule system from her mother-in-law, who had used it to raise her own children. Eldest among them was Jedotta's husband, Brian, who happens to be one of the wisest pastors and Bible teachers I've ever met. In my eyes, that counts as living proof that the three-rule system produces results. Granted, the goal for your kids and mine may not be a lifelong career in theology—God would first have to convince my eight-year-old daughter to give up her dream of becoming a zookeeper. But every child raised in a Christian home can certainly grow up to make an impact for the kingdom of God. As moms we pour our hearts into preparing them for that life mission. The three-rule system helps.

The concept is ridiculously simple and soundly biblical. Concentrate on three core family rules, which everyone can remember. But make those rules broad enough so that nearly every behavior is encompassed within.

Here are our three.

Rule #1: Obey the First Time

Have you ever told your child to turn off the TV, returned thirty seconds later to discover she was still parked in the same beanbag chair, so you repeated your instruction about six hundred more times before the sweet creature finally decided to comply?

Yep. Me too.

But it's not a very effective method, is it? Because not only does this command–ignore cycle do nothing to build the child's character, it also erodes our authority as moms and drives a good woman's temper straight up the cranky meter.

Children need to learn an important truth about God: *Delayed obedience is disobedience.*

Obedience is God's idea. According to the *International Standard Bible Encyclopedia*, "Obedience is the supreme test of faith in God and reverence for Him."[1] It means doing what He tells you to do, when you're told to do it—whether you agree with the command or not. Anything less is disqualified. It doesn't fit the definition. This expectation was set long ago, from the beginning of time.

> The Lord God took the man and put him in the Garden of Eden to work it and take care of it. And the Lord God commanded the man, "You are free to eat from any tree in the garden; but you must not eat from the tree of the knowledge of good and evil, for when you eat from it you will certainly die."
>
> Genesis 2:15–17

Of course, you may recall "the man" chose to disobey that little command, which led to sin polluting the entire world and ultimately trickling down into us and our children—which is why we need a Cranky Mom Fix in the first place. Thanks a lot, Adam and Eve.

However, let's not miss the first verse of that passage: "The Lord God took the man and put him in the Garden of Eden to work it and take care of it" (Genesis 2:15). Before God punished Adam and Eve for their disobedience, He gave them a compelling reason to obey. He gave them paradise. He is a good and generous Father! They *chose* to risk it all by disobeying His command. And God had to follow through because He cannot be a liar.

Does that mean God doesn't give second chances? Of course He does. That's what Jesus is all about. God established His plan to restore humanity even before Adam and Eve sinned. He knew His kids would mess up. He knew we'd need His mercy. And our children need ours, too. We'll talk more about that in the pages to come.

But understand—obedience is still an expectation for the Christian life.

> The one who has contempt for instruction will pay the penalty, but the one who respects a command will be rewarded.
>
> Proverbs 13:13 HCSB

What does this mean for our kids? Obeying God involves obeying the people He put in charge of them, namely, Mom and Dad. Their job is to obey our commands—the first time.

Wash your hands for dinner means wash your hands for dinner—now, not after I've told you three times.

Put your socks in the hamper means put your socks in the hamper—yes, you. Bribing your brother to do it for you doesn't count.

And *clean the bathroom before I get home from running errands* means clean the stinking bathroom—*before* I get home, not as I'm walking in the door while you jump off the couch like you've been just about to scrub the toilet all along.

Teaching our kids to obey is one of the most important jobs we have as parents. However, I need to remind us of a few important caveats that we've explored so far in this book.

——————— Obey Fast ———————

For young children ages three and under, rather than telling them to obey the first time, try saying "obey fast." They know what *fast* means, and it becomes a fun game to see just how fast they can follow through on an instruction to pick up their toys, settle in for a nap, and so on.

- Recall that Ephesians 6:4 warns us not to "exasperate" our children. We shouldn't expect our kids to obey cruel or unreasonable demands. As parents, we have a responsibility to deliver our instructions with love and peace, for the purpose of teaching, protecting, and encouraging our sons and daughters. Be sure to employ the strategies we learned in chapter 7, such as giving a five-minute warning, and not making the kids your slave.

- If your child does not obey the first time, assess the mind-will-heart connection to determine if an emotional obstacle needs attention.

- And finally, our children belong to God first. They are obligated to obey their heavenly Father—and we should never ask our children to sin against Him. God has harsh words of warning for anyone who tries.

But if you cause one of these little ones who trusts in me to fall into sin, it would be better for you to be thrown into the sea with a large millstone hung around your neck.

Mark 9:42 NLT

Many children will struggle to obey the first time, especially if you haven't enforced this expectation in the past. Anticipate they might falter at first and as phases of childhood come and go. That's why we need the rule, really—as a constant reminder of the goal. And what is the goal? It's not just to generate good behavior. Underneath all the instructions and commands we throw at our kids, obedience has a much greater purpose.

It shows God how much we love Him. And *that* is a pursuit worth chasing for a lifetime.

If you love me, keep my commands.

John 14:15

Rule #2: No Disrespectful Talk

Choose your adjective here—no disrespectful talk, no back talk, no sassy talk. The point is to set the expectation that our words, body language, and facial expressions should not show or suggest disrespect to another person—especially to Mom and Dad. This rule is super handy because it encompasses any type of communication that could be considered insulting, crass, or insolent—including quarreling, cussing, rolling eyes, and about a dozen different inflections of the word *whatever*.

> Do not let any unwholesome talk come out of your mouths, but only what is helpful for building others up according to their needs, that it may benefit those who listen.
>
> Ephesians 4:29

Another way to explain this rule to our kids is to teach them the difference between building up and tearing down—especially when interacting with one another. I often ask my girls, "Did what you just said to your sister encourage her or discourage her? Did it build her up or tear her down?" We need to help our children discern between kind words and hurtful words. Unfortunately, many popular kids' TV shows today feature siblings poking fun at one another, arguing with their parents, or making sarcastic remarks to get a laugh. If that's what the world says is normal, then let's inspire our kids to be different.

> Therefore encourage one another and build each other up, just as in fact you are doing.
>
> 1 Thessalonians 5:11

Rule #3: No Hurting Someone on Purpose

Our third rule is just plain genius. "No hurting someone on purpose" covers every kind of hurt—physical and emotional. No more specifying a hundred harmful actions such as kicking, biting, hitting, tripping, name-calling, belittling, ignoring, and so on. Basically, if your behavior is meant to hurt somebody, it's not allowed.

> Get rid of all bitterness, rage and anger, brawling and slander, along with every form of malice. Be kind and compassionate to one another, forgiving each other, just as in Christ God forgave you.
>
> Ephesians 4:31–32

What I especially love about this rule is the term *on purpose*, which helps differentiate between intentional behavior and accidents. We have a lot of grace for accidents in our house. If you didn't mean to whack your sister in the head while you were dancing in the living room, an apology is still in order. But since we Kopitzkes freely encourage dancing, nobody actually broke a rule.

"P.S., I Love You"

Now, I know I said this was a three-rule system, and that's enough. However, in our family we do add one more overarching "rule": *Always show love.*

Why? Because that's God's rule, too—and in a pinch it's the only one we really need.

> Above all, love each other deeply, because love covers over a multitude of sins.
>
> 1 Peter 4:8

Three Family Rules

Download a printable poster of the three family rules at becky kopitzke.com/crankymomfix.

How to Enforce the Three-Rule System

As I mentioned earlier, I don't take credit for the three-rule system because I got it from Jedotta, who inherited it from someone else and, well, we could all say we got it from God because the principles are biblical at heart. Since the system was successful in Jedotta's family, I decided to adopt a version of her follow-through approach as well. And I'm here to tell you, it worked.

Keep track. My family used check marks to keep track of each time a rule was broken. I wrote both daughters' names on a dry-erase fridge board and added one check mark for each infraction. If a child collected three check marks in a day, we took away a favorite toy—which was a big deal to my kids. Your consequence might be different; just make sure it's something that inflicts enough "pain" to motivate. Then the next day, we returned the toy, and all the previous day's check marks were wiped clean—because God's mercies are new every morning (Lamentations 3:22–23).

Please understand this is not a "three strikes" system where our children are allowed off the hook the first two times they break a rule. Not at all. The check mark is in itself a form of punishment. It holds the kids accountable every time they break a rule. That check mark says, "I know what you did, and I am giving you a consequence for your actions." My kids did *not* want to rack up check marks. The check mark hurts. Yet it's also a training tool to help our children understand what types of behavior are associated with each rule.

Train. Sometimes kids may not even realize their behavior counts as sassy or hurtful. So I used the check marks to point out misbehavior and explain why it was wrong. This is also a sanity-saver for those of us moms who feel like we're punishing our kids all day long. By focusing more on training than penalizing, we help our kids make better choices *and* cut the serious consequences down to a third.

One caution flag: If your child does something extreme or dangerous to himself or others, you can jump right to the consequence.

A friend of mind once found her toddler holding a butcher knife in the kitchen. The poor kid might not have realized this was a bad idea, but as soon as her mom gently coaxed the knife away, she responded with a swift consequence in order to instill in the little chef's mind just how *not* okay it was to play with knives.

Persevere. Lastly, lovely mommas, please remember, this system is helpful but it's not perfect. We're all going to get tired and struggle to stay consistent. Some days the kids will test us beyond our limits, and each child may respond differently to our best intentions. There is no magic formula for raising disciplined kids—or if there is, I haven't found it yet. Our three-rule system is the most helpful solution my family has discovered so far to simplify our discipline and tie it to God's truth. We used it steadily for two years, and we had some rough days. But now, four years later, my girls can still recite our three family rules off the top of their heads. They own them, they understand when they're breaking them, and we no longer need the check marks to keep everyone in line. I call that progress. Actually, I call that success. Amen?

Let's Dig In!

1. Do you have a long list of rules for your kids to follow? How can the three-rule system help simplify your methods of training and discipline?

2. Our first family rule is "Obey the first time." Why the first time? Read Matthew 4:18–22. In this passage, Jesus has begun his public ministry and calls His first disciples—Peter, Andrew, James, and John. Note how they responded to Jesus' call. Did they say, "Let me think about it," or "Sure, but wait until I've finished catching these fish"? No, the Bible says they immediately left what they were in the middle of doing—the

---

── The Child vs. the Choice ──

Whenever we reprimand our kids for misbehavior, we must distinguish between the child and the choice. Just as Jesus hates the sin but loves the sinner, we ought to tell our kids, "You are not bad, but that choice was not the best." We'll talk more about this in chapter 14.

---

lives they were in the middle of living—and followed Him. What does that tell us about the value of timely obedience?

3. Conversely, let's look at Luke 9:59–62. Here Jesus calls men to follow Him, but each has an excuse to delay. Jesus makes it clear that following Him means doing what He says *when He says it*, without finding reasons to waver. Note that Jesus is not being harsh or uncompassionate. Commentaries on the historical context say the first man was likely in the second stage of burying his father, meaning his father had actually died a year earlier and had already been laid to rest in a cave. What the man is requesting is to go back to the cave and collect his father's bones—a job not worth delaying the urgent work of Jesus Christ. And the second man wanted to return to his family, but keep in mind this might have been a trip requiring weeks of travel on foot; again, we have to trust that Jesus knew what He was talking about when He said the man's request was not worth delaying God's timely work on earth. Remember, Jesus' ministry took place in a small window of only three years.

Have you ever delayed answering God's nudge to obey Him or follow His will for your life? What was the result?

4. Our next rule is "No disrespectful talk." This is an issue of authority. Especially for young children, learning to respect Mom and Dad will ultimately help shape their respect for God's authority. How is back talk a direct assault on this

authority? Why do you think our words matter so much to God? See 1 Timothy 6:1; Psalm 19:14 (note the connection between words and heart!); Colossians 3:8; Proverbs 16:24; Proverbs 29:20; Ecclesiastes 10:12; and Colossians 4:6.

5. Our third rule is "No hurting someone on purpose." Read Romans 13:10; Ephesians 4:31–32; Titus 3:2; and Psalm 34:14. One of the themes we've shared throughout this book is the idea that God made each family a team; therefore, we should support one another and seek the best for each other. First Corinthians 13:7 says, "love always protects." Ask your kids—are you protecting each other? Or hurting each other? Then ask yourself the same question.

6. Why is training such an important component in parenting? How does the check mark consequence help us train and discipline our children simultaneously?

7. See 1 John 3:1; Romans 8:15–16; John 16:27; Matthew 7:9–11; and Luke 12:32. What is the thread running through all of these verses? *God is our heavenly Father.* We want our children to know Him and trust Him. One big step we can take in giving our children a positive model for respecting their heavenly Father is to respect their earthly father. How are you doing in this area? Pray for God to set your heart right if necessary. Respect for your husband shows respect for the Lord.

8. First Peter 4:8 says "love covers over a multitude of sins." What does that mean to you? The New International Reader's Version (a great translation for kids in elementary school) says, "Most of all, love one another deeply. Love erases many sins by forgiving them." *The Message* paraphrase says, "Love each other as if your life depended on it. Love makes up for practically anything." Think about that. Isn't this concept the very picture of Jesus? See Ephesians 2:4–5. We were "dead in transgressions," yet God sent His Son to save us—why? "Because of his great love for us." Love does indeed cover over all sins. How can you live out this truth in your home?

12

How to Discipline with Grace

Of all the hats we wear as moms, my least favorite is referee. Some days it seems I have no chance to enjoy my children because all my energy is spent on mediating their squabbles. You, too? Maybe you can relate to this story—a typical scene from my daughters' younger years.

"Moooooom! She pinched me!" My firstborn, age five at the time, stood pointing at her little sister, the accused.

"She! Took! My! Bear!" My two-year-old sputtered her defense.

"Did you take your sister's bear?" I raised my brows at big sis.

"No. I had it first!" Sure, that old trick.

"Did you pinch your sister?" I knelt to my toddler's eye level.

"Yes." Love the honest stage, don't you?

"You know the rules, girls. In our family, we show love. That means we share toys and we do not pinch. Both of you—to your rooms for a time-out." My verdict was swift and final.

"Nooooooooooo! Waaaaaaaaaaaaahhhhhhh!" My toddler flung her whole body onto the carpet and pounded fists into the floor. Big sister's face glowed red and contorted into desperate wails.

Such cruel and unusual punishment! As though the whole ordeal had been my fault in the first place.

Oh, and did I mention it was only seven in the morning? The girls had been awake and breathing each other's air for approximately five minutes. Lord, help me.

Sometimes I'm tempted to let natural consequences reign and leave my children to battle it out until one of them gives in or loses a chunk of hair. But in younger stages of childhood, and even now into the tween years, they still need my intervention much of the time. My challenge is to stay strong and consistent.

And what a challenge it is.

In chapter 9 we discussed how "no discipline seems pleasant at the time, but painful. Later on, however, it produces a harvest of righteousness and peace for those who have been trained by it" (Hebrews 12:11). If harvest is the result, then discipline must be like gardening. Many of us moms are in the seed planting stage. Some days we can't see anything but a mound of dirt.

Yet God is giving life to those seeds beneath the surface. As our children grow, we'll detect sprouts, and we'll continue to water and weed. Then one day, I pray our sons and daughters will stand tall, beautiful, and unwavering as sunflowers because they'll be rooted in the soil we tilled with our own sweat and prayers, nourished by the shining rays of God's grace.

Oh, how we all need His grace.

Here are four ways to approach our children's behavior with gentle hands and hearts tuned to Jesus. No crankiness required.

Be a Shepherd, Not a Cattle Prod

Sometimes the most effective discipline is no discipline at all. It's true. Remember, the goal is not just to change our children's behavior; it's to draw them closer to God. And responding with grace rather than punishment is one of the best ways we can show Jesus to our kids. My friend Rachel discovered this the night before a big assignment was due.

My daughter waited until the last week to do her quarterly book report for school. And by that I mean she still had to finish reading the book, and then she was up until 10:15 putting the poster together the night before the deadline. That was way past her usual bedtime—and mine! With our packed schedule, I knew this was going to happen. This time, though, unlike previous reactions, I took a deep breath, asked how I could help, and we finished the project together. It was a little way I was able to show her I am on her side, even if she should have read earlier and planned better. Because honestly, who really cares about the book report? Her heart was more important at that moment. She will remember being encouraged and helped, rather than remembering her mom being frustrated with her.

Of course, there's a fine line between grace and negligence. We can't overlook an offense every time if we hope to grow a child's character. They need training and discipline, yes. But you know what they need even more?

Kindness.

A couple years ago, I realized I'd gotten into the habit of doing life with my kids, but not actually *breathing* life into them. And my older daughter got the added pressure of being, well, older—so I'd remind her it was high time she figured out how to be responsible, to pick up her paper scraps and put her shoes where they belong. Most days I followed her around the house barking and jabbing like a cattle prod.

Don't leave those books there. I just cleared the table.

Please stop cracking your knuckles, it's a terrible habit.

Do your homework—then practice piano then study your verses then help your sister put her pajamas on and NO, there's no time left for making bracelets before bed. Can't you see we're on a schedule here?

By the end of a long day, I'd done nothing but poke my precious girl in the back with commands, corrections, criticism, and complaints.

I treated her as a creature to be tamed rather than a tender soul to be nurtured.

And my heart ached.

He tends his flock like a shepherd: He gathers the lambs in his arms and carries them close to his heart; he gently leads those that have young.

Isaiah 40:11

Jesus is the Good Shepherd. He gently leads us, the parents, and He carries our children close to His heart. He doesn't poke or prod, bark or bite. He guides us with kindness, patience, and affection.

Shouldn't our kids deserve the same from us?

I encourage you to try something crazy. Choose one day to lay off your kids entirely. No barking, no commanding. No mindless correcting. Just let them be who they are, without their mother's constant input. I've done this. And you know what? My kids were a joy to be around. We laughed more. We hugged longer. And the house did not fall apart, can you believe that?

I'll tell you what did fall apart.

The tension in my shoulders. The sighs in my lungs. The frustration in my voice—it all dissipated and blew away. Because it turns out nurturing is a lot more enjoyable than taming. And all it took was this one simple shift in perspective.

I am a shepherd, not a cattle prod.

And so are you.

Talk to Jesus

As a shepherd, gentleness and grace become the defining characteristics of our discipline—even when a child's choices still require correction. How? By pointing the child not just to Mom's grace, but directly to God's.

"I can't take credit for this. It was totally the Holy Spirit's prompting." My friend Amanda opened our phone call with those words, and I was intrigued. She explained how her oldest daughter, when she was five or six years old, had gotten into a habit of lying.

"We would ask her, 'Laila, did you brush your teeth?' 'Yep.' But she hadn't. 'Laila, did you take a piece of candy?' 'Nope.' But she had. It was a string of little lies that just kept adding up, and we were so frustrated," Amanda said. "We didn't know what else to do, so we'd punish her."

Laila's weary parents tried everything—taking breaks, with-holding privileges. "You name it, we tried it," Amanda said. "We told her over and over that lying was wrong, it wasn't what God wanted from her. Basically, we'd make her feel bad. And nothing was working."

Then one evening Amanda caught Laila standing near her dad-dy's nightstand, looking suspicious. "I saw an empty wrapper, and I knew she had taken candy from my husband's stash." So Amanda asked, "Did you take a piece of candy?" And Laila said no.

"I was so upset, I took a deep breath and I just stood there and I asked the Lord, *Why is she lying? How can I get through to her?* And literally in my heart—I believe it was the Holy Spirit speaking to me—I heard Him say, 'Have her bring it to me.'"

So she did.

Amanda turned toward her daughter. "Honey, we're going to do something. We're going to get down on our knees, and I want you to tell Jesus whatever you need to tell Him. God will forgive you for anything, honey."

Laila looked at her mom, unsure yet clearly relieved. And what she said next has stuck with Amanda ever since.

"Mom, will you go first?"

"And there we were, kneeling right there on my bedroom floor, facing each other, and I started bawling," Amanda said. "I prayed, 'Lord, forgive me, for being so angry, for yelling at Daddy this morning, for all the mistakes I've made . . .' I just gave it all to God."

And Laila followed.

"She asked God to forgive her for lying to Mommy and Daddy," Amanda said. "Everything she wouldn't confess to us, she confessed to Him. She asked forgiveness for other things, too—things we didn't even know about. And she cried, and we hugged, and we just wept together before the Lord. I said, 'Honey, doesn't that just feel so good to give all your burdens to God?' And I'm telling you—lying hasn't been an issue with Laila since."

As parents, we often experience tension between knowing we're called to train yet also to be a vessel of God's grace. How do we find the balance?

"I'm realizing that sometimes there's no punishment or consequence that's going to solve the problem," Amanda said. "Just talk to Jesus. Invite the child to be with Him, to tell Him what's hard, to ask for help. When I don't know what to do or say about it, Jesus does. He can do what we parents can't."

> If any of you lacks wisdom, you should ask God, who gives generously to all without finding fault, and it will be given to you.
>
> James 1:5

Ultimately, teaching our children to talk to Jesus—to turn to Him when they're burdened or in need—is the greatest life lesson we can impart. He is their source of strength, wisdom, protection, and help. And as our kids go to school and camp and college and beyond, we won't always be there to hold their hand—but Jesus will. So let's show them by example how to seek Him and rely on Him.

"If I get all of parenting wrong and that's the only thing I get right," Amanda told me, "I'm okay with that."

Positive Reinforcement Is a God Thing

I'm a big fan of positive reinforcement. I figure if I can train my kids through rewards, we'll reduce the need for negative consequences in the first place. It's like preventive medicine for bad behavior. Give me a jug of that, amen?

But you know what I really love about positive reinforcement? It's entirely biblical. Throughout Scripture, the Lord tells His people, *If you do this, I will give you that; if you obey, I will bless you; follow my commands, and you will be rewarded.* We can't go wrong adopting God's own parenting style.

Naturally, positive reinforcement works better on some kids than others. You might have one child who thrives on it, another who blows it off, and yet another who tries to manipulate the system to her advantage. But how will you know until you try?

Here are three of my favorite mom-tested, kid-approved ideas for managing behavior with positive rewards.

Marble Jar. I got this one from my girls' kindergarten teacher. Set a jar on the kitchen counter or someplace your kids will see it often. Whenever you "catch" them behaving well (using kind words, sharing, obeying the first time—essentially demonstrating any behavior you want to reinforce), drop a marble in the jar. When the marbles reach the rim, the whole family celebrates. Our family's reward of choice is usually a trip to the fancy ice-cream shop.

Screen-Time Tickets. TV, iPads, video games, computers—our kids are growing up in a digital world, and we need to teach them to manage well within it. Screen-time tickets help, especially in summer. This is how we use them:

- Every Monday, we give each child a budget of ten screen-time tickets for the week. One ticket is worth thirty minutes of screen time or fifty cents.
- At the end of the week, the kids can cash in any unused tickets.
- We allow our children to earn extra screen-time tickets by reading (thirty minutes of reading = one extra ticket) or doing chores.

—— Screen-Time Tickets ——

For a printable sheet of screen-time tickets, visit beckykopitzke. com/crankymomfix.

In summer, our family applies tickets between the hours of eight in the morning and five in the evening. We don't require the kids to spend their tickets on family movie nights or certain educational computer programs they use in school. And if siblings choose to watch TV together, each child has to spend a ticket—no two-for-ones.

When we first implemented this system, my husband and I fully expected our kids to blow all ten tickets the first day. But it turned out the tickets served as a wonderful regulator and motivator. Our children thought twice before asking to watch TV; it was no longer their default boredom-buster. Instead, they had fun seeing how many tickets they could preserve for payday. In the end, our family enjoyed a summer filled with a balance of activities, and—best of all—there was no scolding to "turn off the TV!" Hallelujah!

Redirection Sticks. Sometimes kids need a little inspiration in order to ward off misbehavior brought on by boredom, cabin fever, or too much sibling togetherness. If you sense your child needs to shift gears, try redirection sticks.

Start by brainstorming a list of screen-free activities for each child. Then write these activities on colored craft sticks, one "task" per stick, assigning a different color for each sibling so they can tell whose is whose. Place all the sticks in a cup. Whenever you sense a child needs a break, point to the cup and tell him to pick a stick and do what it says.

The key is to choose activities that promote creative, independent play and physical fitness—to get their mind and body focused on something other than impending frustration. Redirection sticks can help remind our kids how much more fun it is to engage in playtime activities than squabbles—before the squabbles have a chance to escalate.

Now, I know we're talking about positive reinforcement, but, for older kids especially, try throwing in a few chore sticks as a deterrent. Kids may be less likely to get restless in the first place if they know the risk is picking a "mop the floor" stick.

Redirect Me!

Not sure what to write on your redirection sticks? Try these ideas.

Ages 3–5

Look at books

Build a fort

Play with Play-Doh

Play dress-up

Play in the sandbox

Play with cars

Draw a picture

Dance

Draw with sidewalk chalk

Play balloon volleyball

Kick a ball

Make a card

Play with stickers

Stack blocks

Blow bubbles

Play kitchen

Help with chores

Play stuffed-animal doctor

Count your socks

Draw letters

Play with Little People

String beads

Assemble puzzles

Color in coloring books

Run in the backyard

Play with dolls

Swing on the playset

Make something with paper and glue

Ages 6–9

Read a book

Build a fort

Make a bracelet

Build a car track

Play in the sandbox
Write a story
Draw a picture
Dance
Draw with sidewalk chalk
Write a letter to your
  grandparents
Make an obstacle course in
  the yard
Create something with Legos
Practice math
Read your Bible

Make something with paper
  and glue
Ride a bike
Play a board game
Take pictures
Do a word search
Do cartwheels or flips in the
  yard
Make a bead necklace
Assemble puzzles
Color in coloring books
Write a poem or song
Jump rope

Ages 10 and Up

Read a book
Call a friend
Make a bracelet
Sweep floors
Clean mirrors
Write a story
Draw
Dance
Pull weeds
Wash windows
Write a letter to your
  grandparents
Make an obstacle course in
  the yard
Shoot hoops
Create something with
  Legos

Scrub sink
Read your Bible
Do a crossword puzzle
Bake something
Ride a bike
Play a board game
Take pictures
Fold laundry
Do cartwheels or flips in the
  yard
Make a bead necklace
Assemble puzzles
Dust
Write a poem or song
Vacuum
Rollerblade
Skateboard

Biblical Alternatives to Spanking

I'm not a spanker. Personally, I've never found spanking to be an effective solution for my kids. Even parents who do choose to spank, though, would likely agree that spanking is not always the

—— **Positive or Negative?** ——

What's the difference between positive and negative reinforcement? Both methods are meant to motivate good choices and deter bad ones. Which method you choose may depend on the child or the situation. Both methods are supported in Scripture.

Positive reinforcement involves rewarding our children for obeying. Many times throughout the Bible, God says, *If you do this, then I will reward you.* For example, see Psalm 19:9–11; Malachi 3:10; Ephesians 6:2–3; Matthew 6:6; Luke 6:35; and Luke 6:38. We want to teach our children the true reason to obey—the best motivator—is our love and awe for God. We obey because of who He is, not what He can give us. Scripture confirms this. See Matthew 5:8; John 14:23; James 4:8; and James 4:10. God's primary reward for good behavior is to give us more of himself. He is the reward.

Negative reinforcement involves punishing our children for disobeying. See Hebrews 12:5–11. God is full of grace, yet sometimes He disciplines us for our own good. This is an act of love, as Scripture affirms in Proverbs 13:24; 19:18; 23:13–14; 29:15; and 29:17.

No matter which method you choose, make sure your underlying motive is love for your child and for God. Just as the Bible demonstrates both positive and negative reinforcement, perhaps the best approach is to use a combination of each. Remember, we're in this for eternity. Ultimately, our goal in training our kids (Proverbs 22:6) is to one day release God-honoring adults into the world.

best answer. Just as in court the punishment must fit the crime, different discipline situations call for different actions. Here are four biblical alternatives to spanking that can make a lasting impact on your child's heart—rather than her bottom.

1. Nose and toes to the wall. When our kids were small and prone to tantrums, my husband and I made them stand facing a wall with their nose and toes touching the surface, just for a few minutes. This forced them to calm down and focus on something other than their naughty attitude. (Do you know how much concentration it takes to keep your nose and toes against a wall?) Think of it as a lesson in self-control.

> Everyone who competes in the games goes into strict training. They do it to get a crown that will not last, but we do it to get a crown that will last forever.
>
> 1 Corinthians 9:25

Understand, though, the purpose is to isolate but not humiliate. We never did nose and toes to the wall in front of company, and never in public. It's a private discipline meant to remove your child from the context of her bad behavior or overwhelming emotions, and to experience a consequence for poor choices. Nose and toes is a deterrent, just like spanking, minus the whooping.

2. Revoke privileges. We've already discussed how again and again in the Bible, God says *if you do this, you will be rewarded.* Likewise, He also warns that if we do not follow His commands, there will be consequences. Parents can follow this model by rewarding good behavior and revoking privileges for bad behavior. In our house, we take away favorite toys or—*gasp!*—screen time. Cruel, cruel parents! But it works.

Every once in a while, however, my husband and I give the kids a "grace pass" from punishment, and I encourage you to do the same. Why? Because we're new-covenant parents, not legalists. It's important to also model mercy and unconditional love, which Jesus grants us in abundance.

Out of his fullness we have all received grace in place of grace already given.

John 1:16

3. *Prayer.* Now that our girls are older, rather than sending them to the wall, I send them to their room to pray about the struggle in their hearts. This is not meant to teach them that prayer is a punishment—far from it. My kids know prayer is a privilege, and their response to life's problems should be to reconnect with the One who loves and empowers them to see themselves the way God sees them. They usually come out apologizing, and even smiling.

Submit yourselves, then, to God. Resist the devil, and he will flee from you.

James 4:7

4. *Take the hit.* There's a legendary story shared in my church about one of our former pastors. His children had gotten into big trouble, and his wife turned to Dad to deliver the punishment. But instead of giving their kids the spanking, our pastor took it for them.

Never lose sight of the opportunity to teach your children the true meaning of grace. It will make a far greater impact than a spanking ever could.

He personally carried our sins in his body on the cross so that we can be dead to sin and live for what is right. By his wounds you are healed.

1 Peter 2:24 NLT

And Now for the Rest of the Story

Remember my daughters' quarrel at the start of this chapter? Well, after about twenty minutes of sequestering, my five-year-old poked her head through her bedroom doorway.

"Mom, can I come out of my room now?"

"Me too, Mommy?" my little one chimed.

"Yes, girls. Come here, please." I perched them both on my lap. "What did you do that was naughty?"

"We didn't share," big sister whispered.

"I pinch! Naughty!" my toddler shouted. I tried not to crack a giggle.

"What do you need to say to each other?"

"I'm sorry."

"I sow-ee, too."

They hugged. My heart melted.

Then the little one yanked her sister's hair and we started all over again.

Yes, moms, let's keep planting those seeds, for the love of sunflowers and all things green and grassy. It's what we do, and it's why we need Jesus so desperately—to give us wisdom and patience and freedom from the sin nature that sometimes wants to scream and hide where no children can reach us.

Never, ever, ever forget—we are producing a harvest of righteousness. I witness glimpses of it now. At ages twelve and nine, my kiddos still need a lot of planting but they're also starting to bloom. I see Jesus in them. It's the most rewarding experience a mom can hope for. So no matter what season you're in, all this planting and correcting and discipline and weeding—it's worth every ounce of energy and heartache. It really, truly is.

> Let us not become weary in doing good, for at the proper time we will reap a harvest if we do not give up.
>
> Galatians 6:9

——— 31 Creative Solutions ———
to 7 Parenting Problems
For Moms of Young Kids

Need more creative ideas for handling the kids' wacky behavior? Here's a list of suggestions crowd-sourced by real moms.

Subduing Tantrums

- Hold the child's hands, get down on his level, and whisper, "If you stop, we can hug it out." Sometimes kids will have worked themselves into a tizzy beyond their ability to stop, in which case you can still hug them tight and whisper soothing words in their ears, even if they squirm. Sometimes what our kids really need is security and affection in order to calm down.

- Use a code word. For example, "code red" or even something silly like "watermelon" means: "Your behavior is about to get out of hand, and if you do not calm down, there will be consequences." This works best for older kids who have more ability to self-regulate their emotions than toddlers do.

Sibling Fights

- Make the kids huddle together inside one oversized shirt until they work it out. (Daddy's old T-shirts work great for this.) Chances are they'll start giggling and forget all about fighting.

- Make them hold hands and say something they love about each other. Challenge them to outdo each other in compliments. Once again, they might end up giggling. ("I really love your butt." "No, I really really really love YOUR butt, teeheehee!")

- Every time the kids bicker, give them ten minutes of yardwork.

- Tell them they can only fight outside. Enforce this in any kind of weather.
- Ask the kids, "Would Jesus say that about you?" Or "Would Jesus say that about your sister/brother?" Of course, the answer is usually no. Then follow up with, "Well, what would He say?" This gives the kids a chance to reinforce their worth in Christ, such as, "He would say I'm beautiful and special and I do not smell like poop."
- As a family, memorize Proverbs 17:17 (NLT): "A friend is always loyal, and a brother is born to help in time of need." When the children act unkind to each other, misquote the verse on purpose: "A friend loves at all times, and a brother is born to hit you." The kids will correct you, which helps them acknowledge their misbehavior.
- When all else fails, ban the children from interacting with each other at all. Send them to separate rooms and prohibit them from playing together. This usually helps them realize how much they actually do want to be together.

Getting the Kids' Attention (without shouting)
- Ring a bell or blow a whistle.
- Clap a rhythm and train them to clap it back. This is a school teacher's trick, and it works!
- Say "Guess what!!!" in a really excited voice. It usually grabs their attention.
- Shout "1-2-3, eyes on me!" And have the kids reply, "1-2, eyes on you!"

Getting Kids to Stay in Bed
At bedtime (for night owls who like to come out of bed after lights-out):
- Use a "bedtime pass." Give it to your child when you tuck her in. If she gets out of bed to get a drink, go to the bathroom, or ask for one more hug and kiss, she needs to give Mom the bed-

time pass. When you tuck her back into bed again, she knows she has already used up her one pass for the night and won't get another one!

- Play special music that the kids can listen to only at bedtime, or have a special stuffed animal they can snuggle with only in bed.

In the morning (for too-early risers):

- Set a timer on a soft light in your child's bedroom. Explain he can't come out of his room until the light turns on. This is helpful for young ones who can't yet read a clock.
- Tell the kids they have two options. They can either (1) stay in their room reading or playing quietly until 7 a.m. or (2) they can come out of their room and do chores until 7 a.m. Either way, you win!

Getting Kids to Pick Up Their Toys

- Do a ten-minute pick-up. Set a timer and have the kids pick up as much as they can in ten minutes. This works especially well when the whole family pitches in!
- Pick up by color. "Put away all the blue toys! Now put away all the red toys!"
- Tell them whatever they don't pick up by the end of the day becomes property of Mom and Dad. They must do chores to earn back these items.
- Teach them to put one toy away before they can play with another. Hahahaha, yeah right. This has never worked for most of us, but more power to the mom who makes it happen.
- For older kids, try this trick for motivating housework (beyond just picking up toys). Display a list of chores. Allow each child to pick one. As soon as they're done with that chore, they can pick the next one. Because most kids will prefer to avoid the "yucky" chores, they'll be more motivated to work fast and not dawdle—so they don't get stuck cleaning the litter box.

Handling Begging or Whining

- Tell the kids, "I'm sorry, I don't understand you when you whine. Please try again." And stick to it!
- When at the grocery store, tell the kids there will be no begging. If they obey and do not beg, they can get a treat. If they beg, no treat. (In other words, the answer to begging is always "no.")
- If kids beg for a new toy, game, etc., ask them if they want it more than ____ (some favorite toy they already have at home). Explain that you will gladly trade their favorite ____ for this new toy. In most cases, they will realize by comparison that they don't want the new object that much after all.
- Start a complaining jar! Every time a child persists in complaining, he must put a coin of his own money into the jar. At the end of the month, give the money to charity.

Getting Kids to Eat Their Veggies (or anything that's not a cracker)

- Make smoothie Popsicles. Sneak in some pureed carrots, pumpkin, or spinach.
- Have crunching contests! Serve raw carrots and peppers and see who can crunch the loudest.
- Demonstrate how delicious veggies are. Eat them yourself and say, "Wow, these are SO good!"
- Pay the kids 25 cents for every day they consume five servings of fruits and veggies.
- Use the "one-bite" rule. (Some families call it the "no thank you" bite.) Kids have to try one bite of a new food, then they're welcome to refuse the full serving if they don't like it. Let them rate the flavor: thumbs up, thumbs down, or thumbs to the side. This becomes a fun game the whole family can play!

 *Let's Dig In!*

1. Revisit Hebrews 12:11. How is discipline an important part of shaping a child's character?

2. Are you more of a shepherd or a cattle prod? What does Isaiah 40:11 mean to you?

3. How can "talking to Jesus" make an impact on your child's heart and behavior?

4. Read Proverbs 19:18. The Living Bible translation says, "Discipline your son in his early years while there is hope. If you don't, you will ruin his life." *The Message* paraphrase puts it this way, "Discipline your children while you still have the chance; indulging them destroys them." Yikes! Do you feel like the pressure is on? Raising children is clearly a big responsibility. Discipline is an important component of parenting, and it will play a big role in shaping our kids. But we must always examine one portion of Scripture in relation to the whole of it. God is not a God of rules alone. He never has been. Jesus came to fulfill the law and to bring us the new covenant, in which grace trumps the law. How does a grace-filled approach to training and discipline help breathe life into our homes?

5. What is the role of physical discipline in your home? Revisit Proverbs 22:15. In chapter 7 we discussed the aspect of folly or foolishness in our children. Now let's dig into the "rod of discipline." This term also appears in Proverbs 13:24; 23:13–14; and 29:15. Many well-meaning Christians, pastors, and parenting experts interpret the "rod" as physical punishment, which in today's world means spanking. While spanking is permitted in a loving Christian home—when it's delivered with the right intentions and in the right manner

(never out of anger!)—it is not the only way to discipline. In other words, Christian parents who choose not to spank are not disobedient to the Word of God. The best explanation I have found on this topic is by pastor and author Patrick Schwenk. Read his full article at http://forthefamily.org/is -spanking-really-the-only-option/.

6. What motivates your child? Are you choosing your discipline methods to match?

7. How is redirecting a child's focus actually a demonstration of grace?

8. Read Galatians 6:9. When we get worn down by constant squabbles, disobedience, correcting, and consequences, it helps to remember we're working toward a "harvest." What does that mean for us as parents? How can we apply this verse to our daily perseverance?

Be the F.U.N. Family

"In every job that must be done, there is an element of fun."—Mary Poppins

13

Are You F.U.N.?

Every once in a while my kids say something innocent yet so pro-
found, it stuns me—and stings. Bad.

"Mom, I wish you were a kid. Because then you could play
with me." My younger daughter expressed this little desire of her
heart one day while sitting at the kitchen table coloring dinosaur
pictures. She was four years old at the time. I stood across the room
stirring muffin batter, and my eyebrows shot up.

"What do you mean? I can still play with you even though I'm
your mom."

"Nope, you can't." She shrugged. "You're a grown-up. Too
bad."

Hmm. I paused my mixing spoon and considered this revelation. Am I really so boring in her eyes? I suppose it makes sense.
We grown-ups cook dinner, wash dishes, pay taxes, and sit still
through half-hour sermons. Compared to dinosaurs and scooters
and playground swings, I suppose we are kind of dull.

Parents must shoulder adult responsibilities, and, of course,
those are important. But who says they have to define our children's view of us?

When my kids were babies, a wise mentor gave me this advice: *Be the fun family.* Play together. Laugh together. Be the parents who willingly venture into a child's world and create a home where your kids *want* to be—so as they grow, they won't go seeking their kicks elsewhere.

How? I call it the F.U.N. formula.

What Is F.U.N.?

The F.U.N. family is an acronym designed to help us "boring old moms" establish welcoming, joy-filled environments in which our children can flourish. In the chapters to come, we'll examine each component in detail. For now, here's an overview of what it means to be F.U.N.

F—Establish an environment of **Forgiveness**. Nobody has fun walking on eggshells. Our homes should be a haven of grace where kids are free to make mistakes and express their true selves. If our children know they are accepted and loved no matter what, they'll be more eager to hang out with us. Recall from chapter 7, we need to be their safe place.

> Be kind and compassionate to one another, forgiving each other, just as in Christ God forgave you.
>
> Ephesians 4:32

U—Do the **Unexpected**. Nothing says "fun" like spontaneity. Break out of the usual routine once in a while and dare to be wacky. Surprise the kids with a swimming pool outing at bath time. Camp overnight in the living room. Escape to a ski hill for the weekend. Eat popcorn for dinner. Unexpected fun builds a legacy of happy memories.

> Therefore, as we have opportunity, let us do good to all people, especially to those who belong to the family of believers.
>
> Galatians 6:10

N—Nurture your child's interests, not just your own. Remember how I told you I'm an introvert? At any given hour, my idea of a good time is curling up in an overstuffed chair to read a book or browse the Internet. My children, however, have this crazy affection for sledding. And Frisbee. And whacking each other in the head with pillows until someone either hyperventilates from laughing too hard or cracks a collarbone. It's not always natural for me to join the madness. But I do it. Why?

Because nurturing my children involves embracing who God created them to be—pillow fights and all.

> Don't look out only for your own interests, but take an interest in others, too.
>
> Philippians 2:4 NLT

I realize that for some of us, kneeling on the floor to play with Shopkins is about as exciting as watching paint dry. Not every mom is wired to enjoy dwelling within a youngster's imagination, and I'm not suggesting we need to do this every day, every hour. Kids should learn to play independently and with siblings and peers; that's a healthy part of growing up. To nurture does not necessarily mean to entertain.

However, sometimes our job of nurturing is enhanced by playing. In chapter 6 we explored how effective training involves supporting a child's natural bent. What a wonderful opportunity we have to fulfill that call by actively playing with our children, doing what *they* enjoy.

Fun as Opposed to Holy . . . or Not

I've been sharing F.U.N. family wisdom with my fellow moms for several years now. In essence, F.U.N. is a culmination of all we've learned so far. Don't be a crank. Be kind. Be forgiving. Be fun! Sounds reasonable, right?

Except one woman didn't think so. She objected to the whole concept—for one reason alone.

"Christians are not called to be fun," she wrote. "We are called to be holy."

Perhaps some of you have harbored that same thought. And I most certainly don't object to the second half of the statement. Yes, God's greatest concern is for our holiness—for our spiritual growth, the lifelong process of becoming more like Jesus. That is Bible truth!

> But just as he who called you is holy, so be holy in all you do.
>
> 1 Peter 1:15

However, that doesn't mean fun can't be part of the journey.

Let's remember Jesus was fully God *and* fully human. Do we really think in all His thirty-three years on earth, our Messiah never cracked a smile? The Bible clearly indicates Jesus experienced a full range of emotions, just as we do.

He loved his friends (John 11:5).

He felt compassion (Matthew 20:34).

He got angry (Mark 3:5 and 10:14).

He wept (John 11:35).

He experienced joy (Luke 10:21) and gratitude (Mark 8:6).

Jesus even had a sense of humor, which a savvy reader can glean from the Savior's lessons on humility in Matthew 7:4 (*You think your brother has a speck in his eye? Check the big, fat plank in your own eye, bwaahahaha!*) and on hypocrisy in Matthew 23:24 (*"You blind guides! You strain out a gnat but swallow a camel"*). Come on now, that's just plain funny.

The word *holy* in 1 Peter 1:15 is from the Greek term *hágios*, which means "sacred or set apart."[1] To be holy is to be different from the world, as the Lord is different from the world. Yes, Jesus *was* different—He was God, for crying out loud! Never before and not again until the glorious King returns will the world see such a specimen, a perfect man who never sinned. Yet He still experienced emotions—including, we can surmise, laughter! So is it possible to be holy and fun at the same time?

I believe so.

Let's look at it this way. If cranky moms are common (which they are, otherwise this book would not exist), then doesn't it stand to reason that kind moms—gentle, accepting, *fun* moms—are indeed a shade different from the norm? I mean, isn't that what we're aspiring to here? To look more like Jesus than we do the Momster? And when we do—oh, just imagine! What a picture-perfect example of being set apart indeed.

That's right, lovely mom friends. Don't misunderstand the power of fun. At its core it is simply a manifestation of joy, which is very much a part of being holy.

> May the God of hope fill you with all joy and peace as you trust in him, so that you may overflow with hope by the power of the Holy Spirit.
>
> Romans 15:13

Five Ways to Make Faith F.U.N. for Kids

Remember from chapter 9 that Jesus is not a killjoy? My kids can testify to that. Our church is blessed with an outstanding children's ministry. On any given Sunday, my children might be treated to a puppet show, an obstacle course, game-show prizes, snow cones, or SweeTarts—at the eight o'clock service, no less. All week long, the kids in our congregation look forward to their next chance to sing and dance and *squee!* down the indoor treehouse slide.

No wonder these kids love Jesus. At church, He's a super fun guy.

But what about at home?

It's not the church's responsibility to instill Christian values in our kids. Church can be a wonderful support resource, but faith begins in the family. It's our job as parents to model and teach biblical principles on a daily basis. So—what if home lacks the fun factor? Are we portraying God as too boring for our kids? Here are five ways we can endear young hearts to Christ by making the Bible more fun to explore.

1. Invent memory tricks. To help my kids memorize Bible verses, we make up our own songs and sing them over and over at the top of our lungs until the verses are committed to memory. Sometimes we dance, too, or we come up with special gestures to illustrate the verse. Try reciting Scripture during a game of balloon volleyball, where whoever bops the ball says the next word. Or write the reference in whipped cream and let the kids slurp it after saying the full verse.

2. Make the most of wait times. Kids get antsy in store checkout lines and traffic jams. Why not turn those inconveniences into opportunities? Every time you get stopped at a red light or have to squirm through a five-minute wait at the orthodontist's office, quiz your kids on Bible trivia. Make it a contest where the winner gets to choose a book or Bible story to read at bedtime.

3. Reward godly behavior. I used to hand out "good girl tickets" when I caught my daughters demonstrating a godly character trait such as obeying the first time or speaking kindly to each other. Once they earned ten tickets each, I took them to the Dollar Store to choose a reward.

4. Send mail. Kids love to get cards, letters, and packages in the mail. Write them notes of encouragement and pop them in the mailbox for your kids to discover and enjoy. Consider subscribing to a monthly care package containing faith-based books, activities, or even snacks—great for college students!

5. Laugh. It's a simple reminder, but sometimes we get so caught up in the rules and routines of every day that we forget to laugh with the people we love best. Showing our kids that faith is fun doesn't need to require a lot of effort or planning. The best approach is to walk the talk. If we parents live a lifestyle of counting blessings and praising God for the joy He brings, our kids will learn to do the same.

> Our mouths were filled with laughter, our tongues with songs of joy. Then it was said among the nations, "The Lord has done great things for them." The Lord has done great things for us, and we are filled with joy.
>
> Psalm 126:2–3

Anytime, Anywhere F.U.N.

F.U.N. can be as simple as turning a dull moment into an enjoyable one. Next time you're stuck on a long drive, waiting for a restaurant table, folding laundry, or taking the dog for a walk, try one of these fun (and free) activities.

The Alphabet Game. Take turns naming objects that begin with the consecutive letters of the alphabet. Choose a theme (for example, fruits and vegetables, animals, desserts, sports) and let the youngest child begin with the letter A (apple). Next person gets B (banana), next person C (cantaloupe), and so on. Categories can become tougher as the kids get older. (Scientific elements, anyone?) Recently one of my girls jazzed up the game with a new version. "My name is Anna, I'm married to Alfred, we live in Alabama, and I sell advertising."

Mad Libs. This classic game can be done on the fly. Simply choose a noun in your head and ask the kids for an adjective. Or pick an adverb and ask for a verb, and so on. They won't know what word you're thinking of until you reveal it paired with their word, which is of course what makes Mad Libs so goofy. See who can come up with the silliest phrase. "Hairy toothpaste. Bumpy toenail. Purple helicopter." Best part—the kids hardly even realize they're practicing English skills.

Road Sign A to Z. Find a word (any word) in a road sign starting with the letter A. Then move on to the letter B, C, D, and so on. Everyone in the car gets to participate, and the object of the game is to see how quickly the whole family can work through all twenty-six letters of the alphabet in order.

Secret Handshake. Create a secret handshake just for your family. Since my girls were toddlers, we've enjoyed a covert communication code that I adopted from my friend Tammy. It goes like this:

- I hold my daughter's hand and squeeze four times, one squeeze for each word, "Do-you-love-me?"
- My daughter squeezes back three times, "Yes-I-do."
- Then I squeeze twice for "How-much?"
- And she squeezes my hand as hard as she can until we both start giggling.

Why Should We Be F.U.N.?

As our kids grow older, they will seek fun wherever they can find it—at school, the mall, or in a friend's dank basement filled with greasy chips and a Ouija board, yikes. We parents can often feel powerless against "real world" influences. Yet no matter what age or stage our children are in, we still serve as their primary role models. It's never too late to be the F.U.N. family. Let's start today, this week, transforming our homes—under our loving influence and supervision—into the hot spot where everybody else with "boring" parents wants to be. Then one day when our kids fly the nest, we can hope and pray they'll possess a foundational definition of F.U.N. and pass it down to their own children. And in so doing, the world will be equipped with more and more Christian soldiers who are *set apart* for God. Amen?

Let's Dig In!

1. The word *joy* appears more than two hundred times in the Bible. The word *rejoice* is also mentioned more than two hundred times. Do you ever feel like joy is hard to find in your daily routine? Have you lost your zeal for the wonder of God? Good news. He gave us a prayer for that. Read Psalm 51:12, and pray those words to the Lord.

2. Read Deuteronomy 12:7; Psalm 149:3; Ecclesiastes 3:12–13; and 1 John 5:3. What do these verses say to you? Is the Christian life meant to be dull and heavy? No! God's laws are not burdensome. He invites us to enjoy this life. Yes, we will have trials (see John 16:33), but we can also expect blessings and joy. It's not just *acceptable* for Christians to celebrate and have fun—it's encouraged!

3. Refer again to Colossians 3:21: "Parents, do not embitter your children, or they will become discouraged." The aim of a F.U.N. family is to create a home environment where your children want to be, so that you can remain their primary influence as they learn to spread their wings in the world. How can embittering our children be counterproductive to this goal?

4. Read Deuteronomy 6:5–9. Practically speaking, how can we apply this passage to our households? Spend a little time brainstorming fun and creative ideas for the following commands:

    - Impress God's Word on your children. (What are some fun ways of teaching Scripture?)
    - Talk about God and His Word throughout the day. (Do you bring Him up in everyday conversation? Do you find reasons to praise Him for every little blessing?)

- "Wear" God's Word on your bodies. (How about making jewelry or writing Christian symbols on white canvas shoes? This is an excellent opportunity for kid-friendly crafts!)
- Display God's Word in your home (wall décor, window paint, welcome signs, etc.).

5. Read John 10:10. Jesus came so that we may have life to the full, or as some translations say, "abundant life." What do you picture when you think of living an abundant life? More possessions? More security? More contentment? More fun?

   Now read the full passage of John 10:1–18. Here Jesus is saying that He is the Good Shepherd because He lays down His *life* for His sheep (us). How does that change the way we read "abundant life"? Could it mean "abundant Christ"? Perhaps this passage is telling us the fullest life is one that has more and more of Jesus.

6. James 4:8 says, "Come near to God and he will come near to you." We get "more of Jesus" by coming near to God. What does it mean to come near to God? In what ways can you do that as a family?

7. What is your family "laughter factor"? Remember Jesus is not a killjoy! Quite the opposite—God inspires glee. So we ought to share it within our families. See Psalm 16:11; Psalm 32:11; Psalm 126:2; Ecclesiastes 3:1 and 3:4; Proverbs 17:22; and Proverbs 31:25.

8. How we *see* and *seek* God makes a direct impact on how our children see and seek God. Study Psalm 119:68; Psalm 145:9; Psalm 31:19; Psalm 34:8; James 1:17; Psalm 84:11; Psalm 86:5; Romans 8:28; and Philippians 1:6. These are just some of the Scriptures that tell us who God is and why we can rejoice in Him. He is worthy of our enthusiasm and adoration! Are you modeling this for your kids?

14

F = Forgiveness

Imagine you've baked an enormous, spectacular cake. Stacks of decadent flavors are layered in creamy, gooey tiers, covered with loads of fluffy frosting and spun sugar candies in every color of the rainbow. You invite your children to sit at the table where this dreamy dessert looms just inches from their chins. Their eyes are sparkling, their mouths are frothing, and they cheer, "*Mom baked a cake! Mom is the best!*"

But then, just as the kids are about to dig their forks into this sticky, scrumptious feast, a slimy two-headed serpent bursts from the center of the cake and sinks its vicious fangs straight into the children's forearms.

Ouch!

Suddenly that cake isn't so delightful after all. Instead, it's hurtful and scary. What was meant as a treat becomes an unpredictable source of anxiety and grief.

All because Mom forgot to lock up the snake.

Dear ones, this is what happens when we attempt to create fun without forgiveness. All the silly games in the world won't bring our children joy if we don't first secure their environment, ensuring safety for their souls. In the F.U.N. formula, I call this "F for Forgiveness," or in broader terms, acceptance, grace, and space for the kids to learn and explore and make mistakes without fear of condemnation.

> The Lord will rescue his servants; no one who takes refuge in him will be condemned.
>
> Psalm 34:22

Just like they can't enjoy a cake that might bite them back any second, our children can't enjoy our company if they feel in constant danger of scolding or judgment. Forgiveness is the foundation of F.U.N. If we get this part right, then the "U.N." has a far greater chance of success.

Let's explore five important principles to follow as we establish a home environment based on forgiveness.

Throw Away the Scorecard

My daughters both possess freaky-impressive memory skills. They can recall details of their earlier childhood that I still don't remember living through even after watching videos of the actual scene.

"Mom, remember when I tripped on the rock at the playground with the yellow monkey bars and I scraped my knee and you carried me all the way to the car, then bought me a root beer float? Remember that? I think I was like, four."

Uh, no.

"Remember the time Dad lost his wallet and some guy found it in the men's room at Target and you joked that you were in charge now because Dad couldn't drive without a license?"

Well, I remember he lost his wallet once. . . .

"Mom, you know how I told you I pinched my arm in karate class? I have a bruise now, look."

"You pinched your arm in karate class? When did that happen, sweetheart?"

"Yesterday, Mom. I told you about it."

"Oh. You did?" (pause) "Do you need an ice pack?"

"A little late for that now, Mom."

Right.

(Best mom ever.)

However, my lack of sufficient memory neurons might actually be an asset in one important regard. It's awfully tough for a mom to hold grudges when she can't remember the offense.

> Love is patient, love is kind. It does not envy, it does not boast, it is not proud. It does not dishonor others, it is not self-seeking, it is not easily angered, *it keeps no record of wrongs.*
>
> 1 Corinthians 13:4–5, emphasis added

Have you ever gotten into an argument with your spouse or kids, and then a few days or weeks later couldn't remember what you'd been fighting about in the first place? Count yourself blessed. The Bible says forgetting is a good thing. If we are going to create forgiving environments, we need to make a habit of erasing offenses and not keeping score. Holding a person's transgressions against them, bringing up old mistakes time and time again, and using those mistakes as ammunition whenever a new argument begins is *not* the way Jesus loves us. Remember, His mercies are new every morning (Lamentations 3:22–23). He forgives our offenses completely and nails them to the cross, never to be yanked off again. Therefore, we ought to love our people that way, too.

> He has removed our sins as far from us as the east is from the west.
>
> Psalm 103:12 NLT

Refrain from Shame

My friend Bea grew up in a household where crying was off-limits. Her dad "couldn't stand tears," she said, so she spent her childhood trying to stiffen her bottom lip in order to meet his approval. "It was a tall order for me, a naturally sensitive and emotional child," she explained. "It wasn't until years later, as an adult, that I learned crying is okay. Being sensitive is okay—even helpful sometimes. This is how God made me and it's not something to be ashamed of."

In our efforts to train and correct our kids, we must be careful not to cross the line to shame. Training focuses on improving a behavior or properly channeling an emotion. Shaming simply says, "There's something wrong with you as a person."

One builds up; the other tears down.

> So let us do all we can to live in peace. And let us work hard to build each other up.
>
> Romans 14:19 NIRV

What does this look like in real life? Consider these scenarios.

- If your child stands at the launch deck of a zip line, the mom who builds up will cheer, "You can do it!" Tearing down says, "Don't be such a chicken!"
- If your teen's first love breaks his heart, a compassionate, accepting mother will wrap an arm around his shoulders and let him sob into her shirt. A merciless parent, on the other hand, scolds, "I told you not to date that girl."
- And at any age, when our children show fear, stubbornness, sorrow, or pride, the mom who shames will berate them for their very human feelings, their unfortunately normal sins. The mom who loves like Jesus will remember that she is a sinner, too, and she will treat her kids with the same forgiving kindness that our heavenly Father grants us all.

> As Scripture says, "Anyone who believes in him will never be put to shame."
>
> Romans 10:11

Apologize

Forgiveness is a two-way street. If we want our kids to live in a forgiving and accepting home, they need to learn to forgive as well. Fortunately, an imperfect mother is bound to give her kids plenty of chances to practice.

"Girls, I'm sorry I whipped your laundry against the wall." These may or may not have been the actual words I spoke to my children just last week. (They totally were.) "I was frustrated that you lost your karate shirts, but that's no excuse to act all crazy and mean. I should've had more self-control. Will you forgive me?"

"Yes, Mommy." My eight-year-old squeezed her arms around my waist. "We understand. You just get crabby sometimes. It's okay. I do, too."

"Yeah, Mom. You're just tired. We forgive you." My lovely tween joined her little sister and me in a group hug, and our peace was restored.

We've just spent more than a dozen chapters talking about how to prevent these kinds of cranky mom outbursts. Yet in the long run we won't do it perfectly. Even a kind and gentle mom will experience an occasional flare-up. When that happens, use it to your utmost advantage. A genuine apology will teach our kids far more about humility and forgiveness than our perfection ever could.

Aim for Honesty, Not Perfection

Speaking of imperfect people, let's pause for a second and remember the purpose of parenting. God doesn't ask us to raise flawless children. He wants *faithful* children. And those may be two very different things.

> He has shown you, O mortal, what is good. And what does the Lord require of you? To act justly and to love mercy and to walk humbly with your God.
>
> Micah 6:8

In chapter 8 you met my friend Brooke, the family-meeting mom. When her son was in third grade, he stole an eraser from the school book fair. His little brother discovered it and ratted him out.

"I was appalled and started to panic," Brooke said. "We teach our kids not to steal, my son knew it was wrong, and suddenly I was faced with the reality that he had done this." Yet rather than dwell on her disappointment or the creeping feeling that she had somehow failed as a mother, Brooke chose to capture the teachable moment.

She sat her son down and asked him to explain what had happened. It turned out a friend had dared him to sneak the eraser into his pocket, so they talked about peer pressure and standing up for what's right. She made her son write a letter of apology to the school librarian in charge of the book fair, and they delivered it in person.

"He stood there with tears rolling down his face, held out his hand, and showed her the eraser," Brooke said. The librarian was

Forgiving Phrases

Our words have the power to hurt or heal. Here are some helpful phrases to use with our children in situations of training or discipline. Each of these affirms godly acceptance even when a child's behavior calls for correction.

"I don't like your behavior right now. But I still love you."

"Let's rewind and try that again."

"What matters is not the mistake you make; it's what you learn from the mistake."

"What did you do that was wrong? What would've been a better choice?"

"Make a better choice, please."

"There is nothing you can ever do that will make me stop loving you."

nearly moved to tears herself and quickly accepted the apology. Then Brooke made a surprising decision.

She returned to the book fair and bought her son the very same eraser.

"I wanted to bless him with it because he did come clean and confess and wrote the apology and faced his wrong," she said. "I am less concerned with his mistakes than I am with how he handles them. We want our kids to know that honesty matters more than misbehavior. If you screw up, just admit it. Don't hide things from us. There is room for forgiveness and grace."

What better way to show Jesus to our kids? When they mess up and fess up, give them a gift they don't deserve. That's the gospel in a nutshell.

Inspire Courage, Not Fear

Do you encourage your kids to try new things? Do they believe they can attempt a new sport, a DIY project, a rock climbing wall, and so much more, simply because you showed them they could?

Expanding a child's horizons can be a blast for the whole family—or not.

"I don't want to go on that. It's too high." My older daughter, age five at the time, tipped her nose toward the sky and squinted at the super potato sack slide. We were on a special family outing to an amusement park, which my husband and I anticipated our kids would love, love, love.

We were wrong.

"How about the race cars, then?" I suggested. "Do you want to ride those?"

"No."

"The floaty boats?"

"No."

"The ladybug buggies?"

My daughter shook her head and stared at her shoes. "I don't like those rides! Hmmpf!" My two-year-old stood in stubborn allegiance with her sister. I heaved a sigh and raised my eyebrows at my husband, desperate to salvage our trip.

"Come on, I want you to go down the slide with me." He appealed to our five-year-old. "I think you'll be surprised how much you like it."

"No!"

Ten dollars' worth of kiddie ride tickets suddenly weighed as heavy as sandbags in my pocket. I grew anxious to unload them. "But you love slides. Why don't you want to go on this one?"

"Because! I don't like things that are high. I'm too scared."

"What's wrong with the buggies? They're on the ground."

"It's too fast. I can't make it stop when I want it to stop. I want to go home."

Trying new things can be scary. When fear gets in the way of fun, our kids need us to remind them what they're capable of: "For God has not given us a spirit of fear and timidity, but of power, love, and self-discipline" (2 Timothy 1:7 NLT).

So what's the secret to raising brave kids?

Be a brave mom.

In planning our trip to the amusement park, I imagined a day filled with cotton candy and toothy smiles. My kids were supposed to squeal in delight and skip from ride to ride while I snapped brilliant pictures for my photo books. Didn't they understand that? Their fears were ruining all our fun.

I know this from experience.

Because I have a few fears of my own.

For example, I fear car accidents. So instead of cranking the radio and relaxing shotgun beside my hubby, I spend family road trips slamming my ghost brake and watching for deer.

I fear germs. So during flu season, I avoid the children's museum and pizza buffets, dreading the inevitable midnight hour when a daughter wakes up vomiting.

I fear letting my children go. So I approach each new school year with anxiety and heartache, praying that God will go with them where I cannot.

What's your list? Do you see? Fears ruin all our fun. They suck the joy from our blessings. We could be belting country songs with the windows rolled down, smacking our lips on a slice of taco pizza in February, or celebrating each child's foray into kindergarten, middle school, high school, and college—enjoying the freedoms that come with each stage.

But many of us don't.

God hands us little tickets to happiness, and we turn them down because we're too darn scared to strap in for the ride.

Mom friends, can we strap in together?

Let's model fearless fun for our children. I want to grin silly and wide until my jaw aches, and feel my stomach plunge down life's super slides. Fear is nothing but the enemy's trap. Let's you and I be determined to bust free.

> Don't be afraid, for I am with you. Don't be discouraged, for I am your God. I will strengthen you and help you. I will hold you up with my victorious right hand.
>
> Isaiah 41:10 NLT

God tells us over and over in the Bible not to fear. Why? Because He knows we will. Fear is part of the human condition. Yet God wants us to remember He is still in control, and He goes with us on the scary rides.

Back at the amusement park that day, I made my daughter a deal. If she tried the super slide and hated it, I promised to give her a jumbo bag of cotton candy.

Would you believe she giggled all the way down that slide?

"I want to go again, Momma!" My sweet girl beamed with joy. I gave her the cotton candy anyway—for bravery. She tackled a fear head-on, conquered it, and received her reward.

And she had a load of fun in the process.

Let's Dig In!

1. Read Ephesians 4:32 and Colossians 3:13. According to these verses, why should we forgive others?

2. Now read Matthew 18:21–35, the parable of the unmerciful servant. This story seems terrible, right? We're appalled that the servant, after being shown tremendous mercy, would turn around and slap a prison sentence on someone else for the same offense. Yet we often do the same thing—to the people we love best—when we demand perfection from our children and criticize or punish them for not meeting our standards.

   Consider this. Are you meeting God's standards of perfection? Of course not. You're an imperfect human. That's why you need Jesus, as we all do. Likewise, your children are flawed mortals, too, and their sins—like yours—are covered by the grace of Jesus Christ. How do unreasonable expectations for our children add a burden that the Lord intended to lift?

3. The NIV translation of Colossians 3:13 says, "Bear with each other and forgive one another if any of you has a grievance against someone. Forgive as the Lord forgave you." The NLT says, "Make allowance for each other's faults." The Greek word for *bear with* or *make allowance for* is *anechomenoi*, which means to show tolerance with patience.[1] Do you show patience for your children's mistakes? Or are you more like a cat ready to pounce? Spend some time praying to the Lord about this. Ask Him to help you pause before you react to a grievance against your kids, and to give you the wisdom to show mercy.

4. First Corinthians 13:5 says love keeps no record of wrongs. Have you been keeping track of all the ways your children

irritate you? Do you hold grudges against them (either deliberately or subconsciously)? Forgiveness can wipe the slate clean and create an environment of acceptance. However, forgiveness is also a daily choice. Reread Matthew 18:21–22. How many times must we forgive the same offense? Jesus says "seventy times seven" not to give us an exact number, but rather a general rule. In other words, He says, forgive time and again. Never stop forgiving. That is the love of Christ in action.

5. Are you more legalistic than laid-back? Each of us is wired with a certain bent toward rule-following, whether strict or lenient or anywhere in between. Yet when it comes to our parenting style, we must be careful to temper our natural tendencies with Scripture to ensure we are achieving an effective and God-honoring balance of justice and mercy. God exhibits both of these qualities equally and simultaneously. Because our job in raising our children is to "bring them up in the training and instruction of the Lord" (Ephesians 6:4), we must remember that Jesus came to free us from the burdens of the law. Discipline without grace is not Christian parenting.

6. See John 1:17; Romans 6:14; Romans 8:1–4; Romans 10:4; Galatians 5:1; and Colossians 2:13–14. These are just a handful of the Scriptures that speak to Christ's purpose of setting us free. How can we apply this principle of grace to our families and to the way we treat our children? Spend some time in prayer, asking God to reveal to you any areas where you have been either excessively legalistic or irresponsibly lenient. Ask Him to show you how to reconcile these two extremes.

7. Do you have fears? If so, how do these fears influence your children? What does it mean to have a spirit of power (2 Timothy 1:7)? The Greek word for *power* is *dunamai*, which means "to be able or capable."[2] How can you encourage

your children that they are capable of trying new things or facing their fears? One of my favorite tips is to stop telling our kids to be careful but instead tell them, be brave!

8. How does parenting with forgiveness and grace demonstrate the gospel in action?

15

U = Unexpected

When you live in Wisconsin like I do, there is really only one vacation destination appropriate for a family of four.

Anyplace warm with a swimming pool.

Recently, my husband and I took our girls to Orlando for a family getaway. We went the first week in June, when local Wisconsin weather held steady at a balmy 65 degrees—too chilly to swim, even for us hardy northern folk. Florida was the perfect place to kick off our summer break. Especially since we didn't tell the girls we were going until the morning we left.

"Rise and shine!" My husband and I tiptoed into our daughters' bedroom and giggled while they shifted under the covers, still groggy at 6 a.m. "Happy first day of summer!"

The girls slowly cracked open their eyelids, not even bothering to sit up as they reached for the envelopes their dad handed them—mysterious letters listing vital supplies for the trip.

"This says we need sunscreen and a plane ticket," our older daughter said, pursing her lips in a suspicious half-smile. "Why?"

"Because!!" I practically squealed with excitement. "We're going to Florida!!!"

It took a few minutes to convince the girls we weren't joking. But once they realized we were really, truly, pinky-swear flying to Orlando in a matter of hours, their enthusiasm burst out in smiles and shrieks and hugs all around. And our family enjoyed a fantastic week of sunshine and flip-flops and way too much ice cream. If you travel often, or if you live two miles from Disney World, then maybe this story is no big whoop. In our case, however, the girls had been begging for an Orlando vacation for months upon months. The biggest trip we'd taken in the last five years was a three-day visit to the Mall of America in Minnesota—in our minivan. We don't fly often. We don't spend money readily. We're not flashy vacation people. But we knew our girls were growing up every second, and we'd never get these days back. They had already outgrown Rapunzel and Tinkerbell. How much longer would our eleven-year-old wish to visit Hogwarts Castle or ride the Minion Mayhem? How soon would our eight-year-old outgrow her giddy fascination with wildebeests and okapis and all things Animal Kingdom? When a rhino crossed our path on the jungle safari ride, I watched her sweet face beam with pure joy.

Priceless.

Our girls enjoyed every minute of their surprise vacation. Together we captured timeless memories and built stronger bonds— all because my husband and I chose to pause normal life and live to the fullest whatever fleeting moments we've been given.

We did the "U" in F.U.N.—the *unexpected*.

Why U?

What's so important about making time for the unexpected? Lots of families thrive on routine and predictability, and there's nothing wrong with that. Personally I love a good routine. I'm organized, systematic, a list maker. I like knowing what to expect, and so do my children.

Yet I also know the risk of routine. It can lapse into ritual, so that we go through the motions but forget to acknowledge why. What is the greater purpose behind our actions? Why do we get up every day to eat breakfast and go to school and work and youth group and soccer practice? Is the work of a family simply to do the stuff, or to do the stuff for a reason?

> Commit to the Lord whatever you do, and he will establish your plans.
>
> Proverbs 16:3

Sometimes the best way to remember *why* we live is to give ourselves a little freedom to truly live. And that just might involve some unexpected adventure.

"Every so often I like to surprise my kids with ice cream and popcorn for dinner," my friend Rachel told me. "Sometimes it's a spur of the moment decision, especially after a stressful week; I'll grab a carton of ice cream at the store and pop popcorn on the stove because, let's face it, it's fun and easy for parents, too. It gives us a break from making dinner and doing dishes!"

Other times Rachel will plan ahead, such as on Dairy Queen's annual customer appreciation day when all treats are half price. "I sneak out to buy Blizzards and popcorn, then I hide them and tell the kids all afternoon that I haven't decided what to make for dinner," she said. "There are usually lots of squeals and 'Really!? Are you serious?!' reactions when they realize what we've planned. Then we all park in front of the TV and watch a family movie for extra fun."

Loosen Up, Woman

Rachel believes her family's popcorn and ice-cream nights hold special value because they build sweet memories and remind her kids that Mom is fun to be around. "I'm usually the drill sergeant in charge of getting shoes on, homework done, and enforcing veggies, fruit, and protein. Daddy is always the fun one. I can't even compete—except on these occasions when we have treats for dinner," she said. "It helps me loosen up and do something I enjoy, too. I take myself too seriously sometimes."

Isn't that the truth? Sometimes we moms can become so focused on managing our families that we neglect to *enjoy* our families. Make no mistake—the "U" in F.U.N. isn't just for our kids. It can boost our own spirits, too.

> Go, eat your food with gladness, and drink your wine with a joyful heart, for God has already approved what you do.
>
> Ecclesiastes 9:7

Do you ever feel guilty about having a good time? Do you struggle to let your guard down and allow your kids to see your sunny side—as if daring to break loose will somehow cause you to unravel altogether, to lose all authority and control? I mean, God gave us this job of raising children, and it's a big responsibility. There's such tremendous pressure to do it right—to train up wise, kind, self-controlled citizens. One day we bend on ice cream for dinner, and who knows? The next day the kids will be running wild down the street—with scissors!

Yep. I can relate to those fears. I have them, too. And that's when I realize—the person who most needs a dose of "U" is me.

> We must enjoy ourselves, enjoy our friends, enjoy our God, and be careful to keep a good conscience, that nothing may disturb us in these enjoyments. We must serve God with gladness, in the use of what he gives us, and be liberal in communicating it to others, and not suffer ourselves to be oppressed with inordinate care and grief about the world.[1]

This commentary on Ecclesiastes 9 was written more than three hundred years ago by a Puritan minister named Matthew Henry.

Even today his words hit me like a rock in the gut. We must "not suffer ourselves to be oppressed with inordinate care and grief about the world." Do you know what that means? In terms of motherhood, when we hold so tightly to our worries, to our "good moms do it this way" guidelines, and when we believe we have more power to shape our children than God does—as if their future is wholly dependent on whether or not we mess up—we suffer. We are *oppressed*. We choose to carry a burden God never intended us to hold.

Never forget, in God's eyes, we are "already approved." Christians live under grace, not condemnation.

So eat the ice cream, sweet mom friends. Do the unexpected. Your household will not fall apart because of it. It will flourish.

What Does the "U" Say to Our Kids?

We've seen how bestowing unexpected blessings on our children can boost morale, create precious memories, and help a weary mom enjoy her family. Yet there's another benefit that goes beyond the fun factor and proves the "U" can be a helpful tool in raising confident kids.

Unexpected blessings remind our kids they are loved.

"My son was outgrowing his little-kid bedroom," my friend Karyn told me. "It still had the original builder's white on the walls, a random assortment of childish stuff around the room, nothing matched or coordinated. I just don't think he ever felt like it was 'his' room."

So while her tween-age son was gone for a week at summer camp, Karyn gave his room a complete makeover.

"He's a huge Denver Broncos fan, so I went with a navy and orange football theme," she said. "It became quite a labor of love." Karyn searched online for the perfect Broncos horse-head emblem, enlarged it with an overhead projector, and traced it on the wall. She then hand-painted the emblem and painted the surrounding walls and shelves in complementary Broncos colors.

— More Ideas for Unexpected Fun —

Pajama run. My mentor Debbie taught me this one. On a random evening after the kids are tucked into bed, announce "pajama run!" and load up everybody in the car for drive-thru ice cream, donuts, or a tour of Christmas lights, and so on.

Surprise shopping spree. Take young kids to the Dollar Store and give them three dollars each to spend. For older kids, consider a special splurge every once in a while (if you can swing it). Surprise them with $50 or $100 and a trip to their favorite clothing or activities store. My dad used to do this with my sisters and me, and those shopping trips are still some of my fondest memories from childhood. (I mean really, how sweet of a dad to take a thirteen-year-old girl shopping one-on-one!)

Surprise getaway. At least once in their childhood, whisk the kids away on a weekend trip without telling them ahead of time when

"It really didn't cost me much more than the price of paint and a few extras to spice up the room, like new sheets, lampshades, and an inexpensive orange trash can I found on Amazon," Karyn said. "I spent a lot of late nights on the project when my younger kids were asleep. I finally got everything put back together at about three o'clock the night before my son was due to come home."

When he walked into his room for the first time, Karyn's son was shocked. "He just kept saying, 'Is this *my* room?? I can't believe it!' and 'I feel like it's a college room, Mom!' His face said it all. He was so happy and just wanted to sit in there and look at everything. I don't think he'll ever forget it," Karyn said.

The best part, in the long run, is what that new room represents. "I felt great being able to give him a gift like that. He's my oldest and often most difficult child, and I'm sure there are so many times he feels I'm hardest on him. But when he's in his or where you're going. My favorite destination is a water-park resort with water slides, rides, and pools for the whole family.

Switcheroo night. Eat dessert first! This one is a favorite in the Kopitzke house.

Standing breakfast. Do you have trouble corralling kids in the morning? Invite them to stand at the kitchen counter or island to eat their breakfast. No sitting required! See who can stand on one leg the longest. The point is just to break out of the ordinary routine and create some giggles.

Opposite day. Let the kids' imaginations run wild and do things you normally would not do.

Love notes. Write notes of encouragement to each child and leave them on their pillows to discover at bedtime. Sometimes the littlest surprises mean the most.

room, he can look around and hopefully remember how much his mom loves him."

From total room makeovers to popcorn for dinner, the "unexpected" part of F.U.N. can come in all shapes and sizes. There are countless ways we can infuse the "U" into our children's lives, to show them we value play time, diversions, new ideas, and not least of all, their hearts. You don't have to be adventurous by nature, nor do your kids. Even children who dislike surprises can benefit from a boost of fun. Why? Because it's not a matter of shock and awe. The "U" is about making time for the people we love best. And Jesus is totally in favor of that.

So then, as often as we have the chance, we should do good to everyone, and especially to those who belong to our family in the faith.

Galatians 6:10 GNT

It's Your Special Day!

Raise your hand if you celebrate your children's birthdays. Me too! Me too! We love birthdays in our house. Cake, balloons, presents, piñatas—birthdays are great fun for the whole family.

But what about "special days"? Do you celebrate those?

My friend Brooke does. And it's one of the best "unexpected" ideas I've heard for showing a child how much he or she is cherished.

"We have a tradition in our family of choosing a day at random for each child once a year and declaring it his 'special day.' Our boys, Kaden and Kameron, never know when their day is coming; they find out when they get home from school," Brooke said.

When it's his special day, the honored child will be greeted with a sign that says "Happy Kaden Day" or "Happy Kameron Day" plus a table set with a homemade cake or cookies, a few small wrapped gifts, and a balloon attached to his dinner chair. Sometimes Brooke makes her son's favorite dinner, or he gets to choose a restaurant instead. "One year my older son requested to play a family game together. Another time my younger son chose to eat out at McDonald's," she explained. "Their requests aren't wild or crazy, and that is what's so great about it. The point is not really what we do; it is just that it's all about them. Our attention is solely on our kids, which is enough to make the day extra special."

Brooke says the surprise aspect is her boys' favorite part. "My two sons love this tradition so much, they even get excited for *each other's* special day."

Another variation on the "special day" is a "yes day." Jill, my fellow school mom, chooses one day a year—usually on trips to the beach, the county fair, or shopping—in which she says yes to everything her kids ask for. The key, she says, is that the kids don't actually know it's a yes day. "That way, you can enjoy their excitement without worrying about them taking advantage of the situation," Jill said. "It's great fun for the kids and parents alike."

That's what it comes down to, really. F.U.N. families do the "U"—for everybody's benefit.

Let's Dig In!

1. In this chapter we explored several benefits of unexpected gifts and gestures.

   - Stepping outside our normal routine can help build happy memories and boost the family morale.
   - A change of routine is healthy for a mother's spirits; it reminds us to embrace God's grace and enjoy our families.
   - Unexpected blessings show the kids we're thinking of them and their well-being. Surprises can say "I love you" in new and memorable ways.

   Which of these benefits do you need most in your family right now? Why?

2. Review Galatians 6:10. The Bible tells us to "do good to all people"—especially the family of believers. This begins with your own family! How can you "do good" to your family today? Think beyond the usual care and feeding routines and consider some ideas for infusing glee into your day. This is what we mean by doing the unexpected.

3. Do you work outside the home? Volunteer at your church? Tend to the needs of your friends or neighbors? Let me ask you a tough question. Are you nicer to people outside your home than you are to the people inside your home? If so, you're not alone. This is a trap many of us moms fall into. Our families bear the brunt of our grumpiness because we know they love us unconditionally and will absorb our

blows in ways our friends and co-workers may not. However, as we've just read, God's Word tells us to "do good" to everyone, especially our families. They ought to stake first dibs on our kindness! Read 1 Timothy 3:5 and 5:8. These verses were written for elders of the church, yet we can apply the principles to our own role as parents. How can you make improvements in this area?

4. Consider again Ecclesiastes 9:7, which says, "God has already approved what you do." What does that mean to you? How can we apply it to our family lives? See Romans 3:28; Romans 4:5; Romans 5:1; Galatians 2:16, 20–21; and Galatians 3:24.

5. Revisit the quote from Matthew Henry's commentary on Ecclesiastes 9. He says, "We must serve God with gladness" and "be liberal communicating" that gladness to others. How do fun surprises and breaks from our ordinary routine communicate gladness to our children?

6. How can unexpected blessings show our children they are loved? How might this help instill confidence and a healthy sense of self-worth in our kids?

7. Are you a naturally adventurous person? Or do you tend to prefer routine and predictability? How can our natural inclinations make it easier or more difficult to do the "U"?

8. Psalm 139:16 says, "All the days ordained for me were written in your book before one of them came to be." God knows the number of our days on earth; He sees our past, present, and future simultaneously. Each day is a gift from Him. How can breaking out of our normal routine to focus on our family in a new or special way actually be an act of respect and reverence for God?

16

N = Nurture

My mentor Cindy is full of wisdom. Several years ago she led an intensive discipleship study that I was blessed to be a part of. There were five of us in the group—all younger moms with babies on our hips and toddlers to chase. Cindy had raised three grown children of her own, and she carried a wealth of experience and wisdom in her heart that she was passionate about passing down to us. I learned so much from her about what it means to be a Christian, an evangelist, and a godly wife and mother. Yet one nugget stuck with me most.

Be a fun family. Do what your kids love to do.

The whole notion of my F.U.N. acronym was sparked by Cindy's encouragement to engage in our children's interests and to be involved at a personal, recreational level in order to build camaraderie and trust, especially as our sons and daughters grow into the teen years.

"We need to build a relationship with our kids if we hope to have any influence in their lives," Cindy told me. "In the long run, our greatest goal of parenting is to see our children loving and living for the Lord as adults. And as parents, we get the privilege of introducing them to Him. So think about it. If my kids don't like me, then why would they like my Jesus?"

The "N" in F.U.N.—nurturing our children's interests—is the final key to creating a home environment where our children desire to abide, learn, and play, and where our positive influence can help shape them into godly people. Nurturing their interests may not always be easy, and it might stretch us beyond our comfort, but it will be profoundly worthwhile. Let's unpack five insightful strategies for doing the "N" in F.U.N.

Pray Over Your Kids

Do you realize your relationship with your son or daughter is not just between mother and child? There's a third party in the mix, who is arguably the most important person involved—God.

> For where two or three gather in my name, there am I with them.
>
> Matthew 18:20

On our own, we parents are just faulty humans. We lack wisdom, especially when we come upon a new phase of childhood and everything we thought we knew flies out the window. (Seriously. There's nothing like puberty to make a mom feel clueless all over again. Heaven help us all.)

Thankfully, God is the source of all wisdom, and He wants us to ask Him for it. Remember James 1:5? We've discussed this verse a couple times in previous chapters, but it's worth repeating here.

> If any of you lacks wisdom, you should ask God, who gives generously to all without finding fault, and it will be given to you.
>
> James 1:5

Wisdom is an ongoing theme in parenting. We need it, desperately. So pray for God to help you know your children—their personalities, their hearts, the soul God fashioned within each of them—and to help guide you through each new joy and challenge. Pray that He would meet your children's needs both big and small, as well as help them "grow in the grace and knowledge of our Lord and Savior Jesus Christ" (2 Peter 3:18). When we invite God to lead our relationship with our children, we can be confident He'll make it stronger. "A cord of three strands is not quickly broken" (Ecclesiastes 4:12).

Ask Questions—and Listen to the Answers

Nurturing a child's interests requires knowing what those interests are in the first place. Recall in chapter 6 we talked about recognizing your child's natural bent and acknowledging that it may be different from your own. Understanding now that your child is a unique person crafted by God on purpose and *for* a purpose, a mother's job becomes unearthing just who that person is—and inviting him or her to flourish.

This process begins with asking questions, and being available to *answer* questions when our kids are eager to talk. Here are some subjects to spark conversation:

- What do you like most about [name an activity you've noticed your child enjoys—golf, baking, drawing, etc.]?
- How can you honor God with that activity?
- How does this [game, toy, etc.] work? Tell me about it.
- What do you dream of doing someday when you're grown up? Why?
- What do you want to accomplish one year from now? How can I help you do that?
- What do you think God made you good at? What are your best talents?
- Are you using those talents to serve and glorify Him?

My friend Amber recalled the day she asked her three children to describe their "best day ever."

"My husband and I were already in the habit of taking the kids on dates periodically, but we typically plan them, and it's usually just grabbing something to eat or going to see a movie together," she said. "Then one day I heard a radio program challenging parents to discover what their children deemed their 'best day ever,' and I was inspired."

She asked her kids—if they could do absolutely anything with Mom, what it would be?

Her daughter chose horseback riding, Starbucks, and playing Barbies. Amber's two sons said swimming, biking, fishing, and picking out a new Lego set. One of them wanted to eat at Subway and the other asked for sushi. "It surprised me how simple some of these things are," Amber said, "especially 'play Barbies.' I can

——What Floats Their Boat?——

Becoming a F.U.N. family involves nurturing your child's interests, not just your own. Do you know what your children's interests truly are? Have you ever asked them? Below, write a list of each child's top interests and then think of ways you can encourage and nurture these God-given passions.

Child's name: _____

Interests	Ideas to support and get involved

do that! I love that each reply showed my children's individual personalities and interests."

So what about your kids? Ask them to describe their best day ever, and, like Amber, you just might be surprised at how easily you can make their dreams come true.

Provide Opportunities for Your Kids to Pursue Their Interests

When my younger daughter was in first grade, I enrolled her in karate. She's a high-energy, agile child who, at the time, needed a little help finding courage. So when our local karate school advertised a confidence-building class for kids, I signed her up, and she was a natural.

Child's name: _____

Interests	Ideas to support and get involved

Child's name: _____

Interests	Ideas to support and get involved

A few weeks into the class, after spending two nights a week watching her little sister from the sidelines, my older daughter suddenly declared she wanted to take karate, too.

Really?!

Back then, my firstborn was not exactly athletic. Piano, crafts, dolls, watching every episode ever made of Kids Baking Championship, yes—that's my girl. But sports? Nah. Wasn't her thing. Or so I thought.

She insisted she wanted to try, so my husband and I let her take a trial month of karate lessons. And she absolutely blossomed.

Three years later, both my girls are on track to earn their black belts. They've gained coordination, strength, and flexibility that I never imagined I'd see—especially in my elder child. Now she's involved in a leadership class designed to train students how to teach karate to younger kids. It's her favorite activity of the week. And I never would have seen it coming.

We need to be open to allowing our kids to try new things. Their natural bent may be an evolving shape, so as parents we ought to leave room to unveil more of God's design. Your son wants to try the robotics club? Give it a shot. Your daughter is interested in painting? Sign her up for an art camp. Yes, I know we have schedules to manage and budgets to work within, and we shouldn't acquiesce to every whim. Yet a wise mom also knows her children must take an active role in discovering who God made them to be. Sometimes it's a process of trial and error. We have the chance to support them on that journey. Let's provide open doors wherever we can.

Transition from Authority to Relationship

Cindy always taught me that different stages of childhood call for different approaches to parenting. It's a progression, really. "When the kids are younger, we parent out of authority. They're learning basic right from wrong and they need to be taught who's in charge," Cindy explained. Nurturing their interests at that stage might be as simple as playing peek-a-boo or taking them to the library. "As they grow older, however, into middle school and beyond, we should parent more out of relationship," she said. "We're not just calling the shots anymore. We're coming alongside them, coaching them, treasuring them, and being someone they can trust and turn to. One of the ways we build that relationship is by finding things to do together that they really want to do."

Dr. James Dobson put it this way:

> Author and speaker Josh McDowell said, "Rules without relationship lead to rebellion." He is absolutely right. With all the temptations buzzing around our kids, simply saying no a thousand times creates a spirit of defiance. We have to build bridges to them from the ground up. The construction should begin early and include having fun as a family, laughing and joking, playing board games, throwing or kicking a ball, shooting baskets, playing Ping-Pong, running with the dog, talking at bedtime, swimming together, participating in sports, getting kids in great churches with good youth programs, being a sponsor of the school band, and doing a thousand other things that tend to cement the generations together. The tricky part is to establish friendships while maintaining parental authority and respect. It can be done. It must be done. It is the only formula I know to combat the dangers that stalk the land. But it takes time.[1]

Ah, time. Here's where the proverbial rubber meets the road. Are we willing to invest our precious time in nurturing our children's interests to the best of our ability?

"When my kids were still in the house, we made it a priority to share hobbies with them and to be involved in the fun parts of life together," Cindy said. "We volunteered at youth group; we spent weekends as a family at the kids' sports tournaments; we went camping and hiking and thrift shopping and played laser tag on Friday nights. We listened to their music and invited their friends over often. It all takes time and energy we may think we don't have, and quite honestly I'm not a huge outdoors person, so some of those activities didn't always come naturally to me. But those years fly by. They're such a small chunk of our life and super important."

One wise decision Cindy and her husband made was to stay up past curfew so their teens always knew someone was waiting to welcome them home. "I remember one night when our son went to the basketball game with a group of friends. Afterward, the other kids went out drinking, but he chose to come home to play Ping-Pong with his dad," she said. "Over the years, it helped him avoid some of the trouble he could've gotten into, just knowing he had a fun alternative in us."

Now that my own children have reached the tween years, I'm seeing the wisdom of Cindy's advice on a whole new level. My "cool factor" is no longer a given. These days I need to earn it. So I try to share my daughters' interests in movies and clothes; I watch their favorite TV shows and stay up to speed on their favorite music. I'm still involved in approving all of these things, of course, but lately I actually attempt to learn the lyrics to the latest Disney Channel musical *and* sing along—when they let me. It's kind of a riot.

At this point some of you might be thinking, *Hey, my job isn't to be a friend; it's to be the parent.* And you're absolutely right. Yet who says those two things are polar opposites? Continue enforcing boundaries and imparting wisdom, by all means. That's what a responsible parent does. But do it with love. Do it in the context of friendship.

> If I speak in the tongues of men or of angels, but do not have love,
> I am only a resounding gong or a clanging cymbal.
>
> 1 Corinthians 13:1

"Our kids need to know we're on the same side, and that we want what's best for them," Cindy told me. "If we make demands without having a relationship, we're just a noisy gong."

Love "always protects, always trusts, always hopes, always perseveres" (1 Corinthians 13:7). That sounds like friendship to me.

Love Your Children More than You Love Your House

Finally, dear mom friends, a cautionary tale for women like me—the neat freaks, the perfectionists, the "I need my space to be tidy and organized or I'm-a-gonna-lose-my-mind" peeps. I so get you. I *am* you. And I've had to learn how to get over it. Here's why.

"I don't know why I even bother." I swept my tired eyes across our living room crime scene and felt my lungs deflate. Cushions were yanked off the sofa and stacked on the carpet for a makeshift fort. Dozens of books, pulled from their shelf three rooms down the hall, lined the window seat. A pink nylon princess tent wobbled in the middle of the floor, where board game pieces were placed meticulously on kitchen plates—the good plates—for a stuffed animal tea party.

That morning I'd spent two hours cleaning the house. Now, half a day later, it was trashed again.

My husband sidled up to me. "Because, honey, if you *didn't* bother, we'd have even bigger piles of junk everywhere."

So what you're saying is—all my efforts are nothing more than damage control.

Great.

But let's look at it this way. What if I applied the same exasperated view to my other responsibilities? Like cooking, for instance. I can spend an hour preparing a meal that takes my family less than ten minutes to devour. There might be no food left to show for my efforts, but it's nonsense to say "Why do I even bother?" because the point was for the meal to be eaten. It wasn't supposed to last.

Maybe we ought to look at our homes that way, too.

Cleaning is helpful. *But it's not supposed to last.* Because just like meals aren't made to look at but rather to consume, a house is not made to admire but to live in.

And if that's the case, then perhaps the bigger mess my family makes, the better I've done my job of creating an environment where they feel free to live, to be themselves, to explore and imagine, to laugh and to play.

It's time we moms join in.

Ladies, I hereby propose a new attitude toward house cleaning. Yes, it must be done. But consider it always temporary. Scrub the bathroom, then let it go. Whatever happens to the toilet between now and its next scheduled cleaning is not our concern. *Because we refuse to love a clean house more than the people who live in it.*

Amen?

What the "N" Does NOT Mean

We've spent the last four chapters exploring what it means to be the F.U.N. family and why F.U.N. honors God and the people we love best. Forgiveness is the foundation; unexpected blessings make life more interesting and relaxed; and nurturing our children's interests—building a relationship of trust and friendship—can do wonders for our witness.

Yet here I feel I need to pause a moment and clarify exactly what a F.U.N. family is *not*.

It is not a child-centric zone. God first, marriage second, children third. (See Let's Dig In! question 1 of chapter 7 for an in-depth look at this biblical hierarchy.) Nurturing our children's interests does not mean spoiling them, prioritizing their demands above our marriage or time with God, or making an idol of our children. We worship God and God alone. Children are a gift from Him, not a replacement for our Savior. We can and should enjoy family togetherness in a manner that puts God first and honors His design for the family unit.

It is not a replacement for discipline. Anyone who objects to the idea of having fun or developing a friendship with their children as they grow older ought to remember that friends are called to hold one another accountable. Discipline is a necessary part of any relationship, especially parenting. How we deliver it makes all the difference.

It is not meant to negate the parent's interests. As I'm typing this, my older daughter is in the kitchen with her dad, helping him assemble homemade venison snack sticks. For real—my husband is piping a sticky mixture of ground meat and spices into red sausage casings and preparing to hang loops of carcass in our outdoor smoker (oh yes, we have one of those). And my daughter—the girly one, no less—is right in the center of the action, hands on the links and nose in the pungent aroma of it all. Yum.

She loves it.

Why? Because her dad is a meat man, God bless him, and she adores her dad. So he shows his affection for her by not only engaging in what she wants to do, but also inviting her into his world, teaching her his methods and passing down traditions, passions, and memories that will one day comprise the whole of my daughter's childhood.

In all this fuss over nurturing our children's interests—valid and valuable as that is, for sure—let's not neglect to also share *our* interests with our kids. That's a true relationship.

That, in fact, is Jesus.

> When Jesus had called the Twelve together, he gave them power and authority to drive out all demons and to cure diseases, and he sent them out to proclaim the kingdom of God and to heal the sick. . . . So they set out and went from village to village, proclaiming the good news and healing people everywhere.
>
> Luke 9:1–2, 6

─── 30 Ideas for Nurturing ─── Your Child's Interests

1. Dance in the living room.
2. Play balloon volleyball.
3. Eat your kids' favorite snacks or breakfast food for dinner—and tune in to a fun family movie while you're at it!
4. Mess fest! Crafts, recipes, science and construction projects, and more—these are wonderful hands-on learning activities that require space, trial and error, and yes, a big ol' mess. Focus on the benefits of the project, not the clean-up to come.
5. Take the kids out to a laser tag or trampoline park. Play along!
6. Karaoke contest—If you don't have a karaoke machine, borrow one.
7. Table tennis—You don't need a dedicated Ping-Pong table; we have a kit that turns our kitchen table into a tennis court.
8. Progressive park dinner—Choose three local playgrounds and serve one course at each: appetizer, entrée, dessert.
9. Baking experiments—Let the kids make up a recipe and bake it. See who's brave enough to eat it first! (This can double as a science lesson.)
10. Water balloon fight!
11. Twister—a blast for young and old.
12. Play board games. We buy new board games for the family every Christmas.
13. Candy hunt—Hide mini candy bars or other treats throughout the house and send the kids on a hunt to find them.
14. Color safari—Have the kids paint empty egg cartons with a different color for each cup. Then go outside and find an item of each color. The kids must place the items inside the corresponding color cup. You could do this same activity indoors in inclement weather.
15. Fashion show—Collect a bunch of random clothing, shoes, hats, and accessories in a laundry basket or box and invite the kids to create the wackiest outfits they can think of. This is especially fun when the clothes are adult sized! Join the fun by creating your

own wild outfit, then have everyone put on a fashion show for the whole family. Create a runway and take lots of photos!

16. Build a volcano with baking soda and vinegar.

17. S'mores buffet—Roast marshmallows over a backyard fire pit and make s'mores using a variety of substitutions for the standard ingredients. Instead of Hershey bars, try Reese's Peanut Butter Cups, Nutella, Snickers, Kit Kat, caramels, peanut butter, or jelly. Or swap the graham crackers for chocolate chip cookies, Thin Mints, vanilla wafers, or gingersnaps. If an open fire isn't an option, stuff waffle cones instead. Wrap each cone in foil and heat in the oven until warm and gooey. Challenge the kids to dream up their own s'mores creations!

18. Play kickball in the backyard.

19. What Is It? Challenge—Blindfold the kids and challenge them to guess what you're feeding them, according to a theme: flavors of Goldfish crackers, ice cream, chips, breakfast cereal, gum, etc.

20. Decorate cookies or cupcakes—with lots and lots of sprinkles!

21. Build forts—inside or outside. My kids always enjoyed stocking theirs with flashlights and books and spending an afternoon hiding away.

22. Create obstacle courses.

23. Catch bugs.

24. Sing your mealtime prayer.

25. Paint rocks and hide them near park benches or playground swings for other kids to find.

26. Invite the kids to make dinner.

27. Attend your children's sports activities, music concerts, school plays, art shows, science fairs, and so on. And consider requiring siblings to attend as well, if possible. Nurturing one another's interests can help build bonds among the entire family, not just between parent and child.

28. Hug! Give the kids lots of hugs and affection—even when they don't "deserve" it.

29. Laugh! Lighten up, momma! A fun family is filled with laughter!

30. Pray. God knows your child better than you do. Seek His wisdom for how to nurture the young person He created. He'll never let you down.

— 30 F.U.N. Family Traditions —

1. Every year, make a summer bucket list. Let the kids choose what they want to do, then have fun checking off the list all summer long.

2. Create a mini bucket list of activities to do over Christmas or spring break. Choose a budget and a travel radius (for example, only local outings) and let each child choose two or three items to add to the list.

3. Choose one night a week reserved for family fun. In our house, Friday is pizza and movie night. Sunday is board game night. Tuesday is family devotion night, and so on.

4. Let's talk holidays! At Christmastime, choose at least one family activity the kids enjoy, and be sure to do it every year. The Internet is filled with ideas for Christmas traditions. These are my favorites:

   - Bake a birthday cake for Jesus and eat it for breakfast Christmas morning.
   - Deliver homemade cookies to the police station.
   - Make gingerbread houses. This is actually my husband's thing. Every December he and our girls turn the kitchen table into a graham cracker construction site. My friend Rachel suggested a fun spin on this familiar tradition—her family creates gingerbread stables instead. Tootsie Rolls make a sweet baby Jesus.
   - Use special wrapping paper for each child. This not only makes them feel extra special, it also helps keep track of which gifts belong to whom!
   - Every year, give each child a new ornament that represents his or her interests or milestones from the previous year. For example, we gave our firstborn an ornament shaped like a piano the year she started lessons. Another year we bought tiny resin pink Crocs to commemorate our younger daughter's favorite shoes. Over time you'll enjoy reminiscing as you decorate a tree filled with sweet memories.
   - Give a gift to Jesus, such as a promise ("I'll be kinder to my sister"), a worry ("Lord, I give you my hopes to find a new job"), or a vice. (One year my daughter gave Jesus her impossible thumb-sucking habit. A few months later, that little stinker quit cold turkey—a miracle for sure.) Invite each family member to

write their "gift" on a slip of paper and place it in their stocking for safekeeping until next year.

5. On Thanksgiving, use a paper tablecloth and provide a stack of markers or pens. At dinnertime, invite the whole family to write—on the table!—what they're thankful for.

6. On New Year's Eve, camp out in the living room. Set up blow-up mattresses and sleeping bags, snack on popcorn and microwave s'mores, and watch fun family movies until the ball drops at midnight.

7. On birthdays, go around the dinner table and ask every family member to say what they appreciate about the birthday boy or girl.

8. Keep a special plate for birthdays and other celebrations. On his or her day, the honored family member gets to use the special plate at breakfast or dinner.

9. Make resurrection rolls at Easter time.

10. Encourage Dad to give the children personal gifts on Valentine's Day.

11. Let the kids decorate the windows with new gel clings for every season and holiday.

12. Celebrate your child's surprise Special Day! (See chapter 15.)

13. Go on regular dates with your kids. My husband and I swap so that each child gets a one-on-one date with each parent about once a month.

14. Every summer, set a goal of biking together as a family to all the playgrounds in town (or within reach of your neighborhood).

15. At dinnertime, ask each family member to share the best part of their day.

16. If you're gone overnight on a business trip or getaway without the kids, hide fun treats and gifts for them throughout the house, with sweet notes attached. Examples—new books under their pillows, a special dessert in the fridge, dollars taped to their toothpaste in the bathroom, etc.

17. In summer, make a game of trying every new or limited-time-only flavor released at your local ice-cream shop. Rate them on a scale of 1 to 10.

18. Attend a family Bible camp once a year.

19. Eat donuts after dentist appointments.

20. June is National Dairy Month. At least once every June, serve ice cream for breakfast. Bonus if you can find an ice cream shop that's open for a fun outing first thing in the morning.

21. Create a blessings jar. All year long, encourage the kids (and parents, too) to capture moments when they were especially happy or received an answer to prayer. Invite them to write each blessing on a small slip of paper and place it in the blessings jar. Once a year, empty the jar and read the answers aloud to your family.

22. When it's time to shop for school supplies, take each child on a one-on-one shopping trip to select their supplies for the coming school year. Go out for lunch or dinner afterward, just the two of you.

23. Do a "test run" the morning before the first day of school. Get the kids up and dressed and ready to go as if it were an actual school day. Then meet friends in the school parking lot for a donut party.

24. Draw pictures on the kids' sandwich baggies with Sharpies. Leave notes in their lunch bags.

25. Keep a notebook of twenty questions, such as "What do you want to be when you grow up?" and "Describe the perfect way to spend a winter day." Every year on each child's birthday, ask them the twenty questions and record their answers in the notebook. Have fun watching their replies change and mature as the children grow.

26. Read stories to your kids at bedtime. Even as they get older, children still love being read to. This tradition will evolve from picture books to chapter books well into the tween years. Choose classics such as *The Chronicles of Narnia*, *Alice's Adventures in Wonderland*, and, of course, the Bible!

27. Take a family photo every year.

28. Decorate your child's bedroom door on his half birthday.

29. Pray together at bedtime.

30. Most important, choose a few traditions that work for you, and stick to them. Do not feel Pinterest-pressured to do everything on this list or any other list, *ever*. Nobody does it all, nor should they. Celebrate what works for your family, and leave the rest to someone else.

Let's Dig In!

1. Read Philippians 2:4. I like the NLT version, which says, "Don't look out only for your own interests, but take an interest in others, too." As moms, we can easily get preoccupied with our adult responsibilities and preferences, yet God has wired our children with their own age-appropriate preferences as well. These two may not often match. Do you find it easy or difficult to connect with your children's recreational interests? How do they respond when you engage with them at their level?

2. Consider these additional Scriptures that talk about the value of nurturing our children's interests, not just our own:

   • John 15:13—In what ways does a mother lay down her life for her children?

   • Galatians 6:2—In what ways do you carry your children's burdens?

   • 1 Corinthians 10:24—In what ways do you seek your children's good?

   • Hebrews 13:16—In what ways do you share and sacrifice what you have? Think beyond possessions to things like time, energy, attention, prayer, and so on.

3. Read Proverbs 17:22. In what ways does the "N" in F.U.N. create a "cheerful heart" within your children? How does it cheer your own heart?

4. Why is it important to pray for our kids?

5. Do you talk more than you listen? Read Proverbs 1:5 and James 1:19. What can we learn about our children simply by listening to them? What can we learn about our own parenting?

6. Did your own parents encourage you to pursue your interests as a child? How did that affect you? What factors do you take into consideration when deciding whether or not to allow your child to pursue personal interests (such as a sport, club, talent, etc.)?

7. What is the difference between parenting solely from a position of authority vs. parenting from relationship?

8. Do you find it difficult to loosen up and truly enjoy your kids—especially if that means sometimes *acting* like a kid? Why or why not? What obstacles get in your way? Together let's pray for God to help us moms live in the moment, knowing He is in full control of the universe—therefore we don't have to be. That job is already taken!

A Mother's Serenity Prayer

Hey, sweet mom friend. You made it. You persevered through *The Cranky Mom Fix*, and here we are at the finish line. If I could reach through these pages, I would give you a hug and hand you a caramel frappé with extra whip because you've earned it, sister. I'm so proud of you.

You're on your way. Can you feel it? You have the tools you need to slay the Momster, to understand your children on a deeper level, to deliver discipline with grace, and to be one truly fantastic super-fun mom. A happier, more peaceful home is within your reach. All that's left now is to answer the big, overhanging question:

Does it really work?

Can the principles we've learned in *The Cranky Mom Fix* actually bring about real change in our attitudes, our perspectives, our hearts, and our households? It's one thing to read about it, to highlight sentences and discuss Let's Dig-In! questions with a group of gals over a bowl of Tostitos and taco dip. Entirely different, though, to walk through daily life, to face those old triggers and try to apply what we've learned in the moments of frustration, exhaustion, chaos, and noise. I get it. I really do.

So I want to tell you one last story.

Last week, as I was reaching the end of this book manuscript and praying about how I could leave you with a final bit of inspiration before we part, I got a letter from a fellow mom, Cyndi. Her children attend my daughters' school, and I enjoy chatting with her occasionally at special events or at pick-up time in the hallway. From all appearances Cyndi has a successful career, two darling twin girls, a devoted husband, and a basically normal existence. Not perfect, she'd say, but not hopeless either. Beneath the surface, I had no idea she needed encouragement—until she told me I'd already given it to her.

With Cyndi's blessing, I'd like to share her letter with you.

Becky,

Thank you for all you do to encourage other moms like me. I had a moment recently that I know was influenced by your ministry and I wanted to share it with you.

Traditions are important in our family. Each season brings its own chance to relish these traditions. So why is it that the traditions we cherish the most can also bring us to total frustration? In this case, the culprit was strawberry picking.

I grew up strawberry picking with my mom and her aunt. I have cherished (albeit blurry) memories of the hay-filled fields, fresh juicy berries, and strawberry pies. It is only natural that I wish to bestow these same simple joys on our girls. So every year since the girls were toddlers, we have attempted to visit a strawberry field and pick our own berries.

It's been an adventure. We have had trips where we spent more time taking potty breaks than picking. We have had meltdowns. We have had muddy boots. But we have eaten delicious fruit and have made precious memories.

Last year our favorite local farm sold out of pick-your-own berries in literally one day and we missed our chance. Not to fall victim to such disappointment again, I stalked the local farm updates this season to make sure we got out in the fields. And then—our local farm announced no pick-your-own this year.

Not to be dissuaded, I planned a visit to a backup farm. Ten minutes into the drive there I called just to check in and learned that they were closed for the day.

Are you kidding me?

Determination set in. This is tradition, and the girls are counting on me!

I found us a third farm. Yes, honey, it is thirty miles away, but today is our window—let's go for it. Did I mention it was 94 degrees?

So of course we went.

Fast-forward to the four of us in a field. One of our girls relishes this trip for the picked-in-the-field samples as much as anything else. Official taster. Best snack day of the year. These expressions get tossed around with giggles until she's full. And then she stops picking.

She just stops.

Hello? You're ten years old now; you need to help with the work, too. These buckets aren't going to fill themselves! We have to finish picking, drive forty-five minutes home, and then there are still hours of berry processing to do. Come on, kid!

I prodded. Her father prodded. Her twin sister decided to pile on. Sighing, I resumed picking, deciding to lead by example. After a few more minutes this is what I saw.

My daughter lay casually on her belly, facedown in the straw between rows of strawberry plants, with her knees bent and her tennis shoes lifted to the sky. Lounging. Just basking in the summer sun, as if she had no worries in the world as the rest of us crouched, sweaty and exhausted, trying to finish the hard work of picking berries—for fun.

Irritation flashed through me like a wave until I heard your words in my ear: Be a shepherd, not a cattle prod.

I snapped out of it and grabbed the camera. From any other lens than productivity, I realized, this moment is fantastic and demands to be captured.

I look at the picture of her from that day and see she is so content. Belly full, she is relishing the beauty in God's creation. She is at peace. And isn't that really what we all wish for—to provide environments where our children are grateful for the simple pleasures? Where they aren't begging for constant entertainment, restless and complaining?

After a bit, she did rally and take our lead. We moved to a new row where the fruit was more abundant and her joy in finding perfect berries could be higher. Together, we filled our buckets.

In the end I felt such a strong message on my heart to be present. To stop measuring moments just by output. Let them be just moments and be in those moments together.

So thank you, Becky. Thank you for being one of the voices in my head on this parenting journey. Your faith-filled messages are such a blessing. I hope it is an encouragement to you to hear the impact you made on our family tradition this year.

Cyndi

I'll confess I dripped tears over Cyndi's letter, because not only could I relate to her frustrations and her realizations, but also because her story is the kind of outcome I'd been praying about sharing with you—evidence that the Cranky Mom Fix is not some feel-good ideal but rather a collection of real, authentic, tested, and tried solutions rooted in God's truth. It works. Give it a chance, and I promise you, it will work.

Before these pages were a book, they were a live eight-week coaching program in which women gathered with me to chat via webcast about the principles you've just learned. We walked alongside each other, encouraged one another, asked and answered questions about God's will for our lives as moms. And their stories were much like Cyndi's. Volatile moments, defused. Maddening scenarios, redeemed. Peace and joy and contentment found— where perhaps it had been hiding all along.

So how will you capture the Cranky Mom Fix in your moments of decision? Let's begin with the following prayer. Read it, memorize it, own it. Tape it to your bathroom mirror, your closet door, your underwear drawer, and your dashboard. Hold it close to your heart as I hold it close to mine. Let's pray this prayer daily and every minute we are tempted to crack. Then together we really will overcome the crank inside us all, time and time again—for the sake of our souls, our families, our witness, and our endlessly loving, always forgiving, wise and almighty God.

A MOTHER'S SERENITY PRAYER

God grant me the serenity
to accept my children for who they are.

Give me compassion to praise their victories,
courage to correct their misdeeds,
and wisdom to know the difference.

Help me to nurture the unique souls
you have created within them,
and give me strength to allow them to shine.

Grant me patience to guide my children,
mercy to forgive them, freedom to enjoy them,
and enough grace to cover even my hardest hours.

When I feel as though I've failed my kids,
remind me they belong to you.

Help me to love them as you do,
one day at a time,
one moment at a time,
discerning what matters most,
and trusting you through it all.

May I be a kind mom,
a gentle mom,
a fun mom,
and a faithful mom.

In Jesus' precious name I pray,
Amen.[1]

Tools and Resources

What Are My Triggers?

Keep track of your triggers. Whenever you're tempted to snap, force yourself to stop and take a quick assessment of your circumstances. What about this moment is creating an environment in which it's difficult to demonstrate kindness and self-control? At some point before each day is done, reflect on your cranky temptations and jot a check mark below for each of the triggers you faced. You might start to recognize a pattern.

Physical Needs
☐ Tired
☐ Hungry
☐ Pain (headache, cramps, etc.)
☐ Illness
☐ Lacking coffee/caffeine
☐ Medication effects
☐ Hormones (time of month)
☐ Too hot/cold
☐ Other:

Environment
☐ Busy/distracted/ overwhelmed
☐ Too much noise or activity
☐ Feeling rushed/running late
☐ Mess/disorganization
☐ Crummy weather
☐ Sudden change in routine/ interruption
☐ Other:

Spiritual Needs

☐ Neglecting prayer

☐ Neglecting Bible reading/ study

☐ Avoiding fellowship/ accountability

☐ Empty tank (not enough "me" time)

☐ Other:

Emotional Needs

☐ Worry, anxiety

☐ Feeling down or depressed

☐ Grief, heartache, or disappointment

☐ Conflict with spouse

☐ Feeling underappreciated or neglected

☐ Job stress

☐ In-law stress

☐ Caregiver stress (aging parents, sick children)

☐ Other:

Kids' Behavior

☐ Whining

☐ Bickering/sibling conflict

☐ Begging

☐ Crying

☐ Ignoring instructions

☐ Disobeying/defiance

☐ Dawdling

☐ Interrupting

☐ Constant requests for help or attention

☐ Meltdowns in public

☐ Irresponsibility/poor choices

☐ Other:

What does MOM
look like when she's . . .

GRUMPY

What does MOM
look like when she's . . .

HAPPY

What does MOM
look like when she's . . .

SURPRISED

What does MOM
look like when she's . . .

TIRED

What does MOM
look like when she's . . .

SAD

What does MOM
look like when she's . . .

EXCITED

What does MOM
look like when she's . . .

SILLY

What does MOM
look like when she's . . .

CONFUSED

Acknowledgments

My heartfelt gratitude . . .

To God—Thank you for giving me my family and my writing ministry. May those two things never be at odds.

To Chad—You make me a better person. Thank you for your bottomless support and unconditional love. And for making me laugh, even when I don't feel like laughing.

To Clara and Noelle—For every time you've given me grace, hugs, and the kind of pure love I'll never deserve . . . thank you, chickadees. You show me Jesus. I love you forever.

To my mom—I honestly don't remember you being cranky. Thank you for being a safe place.

To my mentor moms—Thank you for pouring into me with your wisdom and experience. I treasure you all.

To Amber—Thank you for loving my kids like a true auntie.

To my fellow mom friends—God has blessed me with an amazing group of women to do life alongside. You are each a beautiful gift.

To our mini-church—Thank you for caring, praying, and being my impromptu counselors on multiple occasions.

To my brave Cranky Mom Fix program participants—Thank you for investing in your families, inviting me into your hearts, and helping shape this content into meaningful, relevant messages for moms like you and me. You brought *The Cranky Mom Fix* to life.

To my dear prayer warriors—You do the most important work. Thank you for caring, responding, and lifting me high.

To Heidi Scott and Judy Episcopo—My beta readers, my advisors, my friends. Thank you for holding my hand throughout the writing process and guiding me with your wisdom and insight.

To my agent, Blythe Daniel—This book would not exist without you. Thank you for believing in me and opening the doors. You are a great blessing!

To Kim Bangs, Jeff Braun, and the entire team at Bethany House—Thank you for making *The Cranky Mom Fix* available to every mom who needs it. You are all a joy to work with, and I'm truly grateful for your support, guidance, and expertise.

To the women who invited me to share their stories—Thank you for your transparency and solidarity. We're in this together.

To you, the mom reading this book—Thank you for joining me on this crazy journey called parenthood. I hope you will retain some nuggets from within these pages, and that they will lead to lasting change in your heart. May "he who began a good work in you . . . carry it on to completion" (Philippians 1:6). God bless you!

Notes

Chapter 1 Who's the Real Enemy Here?

1. John MacArthur, "Eli and Passive Parenting," *Grace to You*, June 27, 2016. https://www.gty.org/library/blog/B160627/eli-and-passive-parenting.

Chapter 2 What Are Your Triggers?

1. *Strong's Concordance*, https://biblehub.com/str/greek/4722.htm.

Chapter 3 Don't Snap. Do This Instead.

1. *Strong's Exhaustive Concordance*, https://biblehub.com/str/greek/3893.htm.
2. *Strong's Concordance*, https://biblehub.com/str/greek/3870.htm.
3. *Strong's Concordance*, https://biblehub.com/str/greek/4550.htm.
4. *Strong's Concordance*, https://biblehub.com/hebrew/5674a.htm.

Chapter 5 Self-Care—the New "S" Word

1. *Strong's Concordance*, https://biblehub.com/hebrew/6960.htm.

Chapter 6 Your Child Is Not You

1. Tim Kimmel, *Grace Based Parenting* (Nashville: Thomas Nelson, 2006), 111–112.

Chapter 7 Have Some Respect

1. Gary Chapman and Ross Campbell, *The 5 Love Languages of Children* (Chicago: Northfield Publishing), 2016.

Chapter 9 Jesus Is Not a Killjoy

1. Helps Ministries, Inc., https://biblehub.com/str/greek/3560.htm.

Chapter 10 Mind, Will, Heart

1. Betsy Corning and Dave Corning, *Entrusted with a Child's Heart: A Biblical Study in Family Life*, 2nd ed. (Algonquin, IL: Entrusted Ministries, 2013).
2. Ibid.
3. *Strong's Concordance*, https://biblehub.com/hebrew/3820.htm.

Chapter 11 Three Family Rules

1. "Obedience; Obey—*International Standard Bible Encyclopedia*." Bible Study Tools. Accessed May 09, 2018. https://www.biblestudytools.com/encyclopedias/isbe/obedience-obey.html.

Chapter 13 Are You F.U.N.?

1. *Strong's Concordance*, https://biblehub.com/str/greek/40.htm.

Chapter 14 F=Forgiveness

1. *Strong's Exhaustive Concordance*, https://biblehub.com/str/greek/430.htm.
2. *Strong's Concordance*, https://biblehub.com/str/greek/1410.htm.

Chapter 15 U=Unexpected

1. "Ecclesiastes 9 Commentary—Matthew Henry Commentary on the Whole Bible (Complete)." Bible Study Tools. https://www.biblestudytools.com/commentaries/matthew-henry-complete/ecclesiastes/9.html.

Chapter 16 N=Nurture

1. James Dobson, "Tools to Be a Great Father," Dr. Dobson's Family Talk. http://drjamesdobson.org/mobile-feeds/tools-to-be-a-great-father/mobile-feed-for-dads/2017/11/11/build-connections-between-the-generations.

A Mother's Serenity Prayer

1. Adapted by Becky Kopitzke from a prayer attributed to Reinhold Niebuhr (1892–1971).

Becky Kopitzke answers to "Honey," "Mom," "Momma," "Mommy," and "Hey, your dog is in our yard again." When she's not slicing apples, driving to karate, tossing frozen chicken into the Instant Pot, or volunteering at school, she writes.

Becky has authored two previous books, including *Generous Love: Discover the Joy of Living "Others First."* She is also the writer behind Kirk Cameron's *Family Devo Kit*, a popular monthly feature on The Campfire. On her devotional website, beckykopitzke.com, Becky offers weekly encouragement to fellow imperfect women in need of God's outrageous grace.

Becky lives with her husband, Chad, and their two tween daughters in northeast Wisconsin. Their second home is Appleton Alliance Church, where Becky leads women's Bible studies, sings on the worship team, and hugs half the people she sees.

More from Becky Kopitzke

Most of us want to make a difference, to live and love generously. But we just don't for a million reasons. Using relatable stories, discussion questions, and careful application of God's Word, here are the inspiration and practical tips and ideas you need to see the opportunities around you, reach out, live generously and bravely, and propel love forward.

Generous Love

BETHANYHOUSE